FLYBALL

Training...
Start to Finish

Jacqueline Parkin

Alpine
Blue Ribbon Books
Loveland, Colorado

Library of Congress Cataloging-in-Publication Data

Parkin, Jacqueline, 1958-.
    Flyball training—start to finish / by Jacqueline Parkin.
       p. cm.
    ISBN 0-931866-89-8
    1. Dog sports. 2. Dogs—Training. 3. Ball games. I. Title.
    SF424.P37   1996
    636.7'0888—dc20   95-26629
                                                           CIP

This book is available at special quantity discounts for breeders and for club promotions, premiums, or educational use. Write for details.

1 2 3 4 5 6 7 8 9 0

Cover photo courtesy of: *Brad and Nancy Vokey*
Cover design by: *Betty Jo McKinney*
Layout by: *Harlene J. Finn*
Diagrams by: *John Robichaud*
Cartoons by: *Howard Kadish*
Text photos taken by the author except as noted.

Printed in the United States of America.

D edicated to the memory of Mickey-Finn (June 4, 1979 to March 28, 1992), without whom I would never have become involved with the sport of flyball, and to my parents for their support and encouragement during the writing of this book.

> Trophy and cup in the cottage stand
> Triumphs you won o'er the best
> But what shall they solace that lonely hand
> Mickey-Finn, that your tongue caressed?
>
> Over your grave as the night-dews fall
> Will they bring you a memory kind and true
> Of the one who loved you better than all
> And faced the world with her pride of you?
>
> > —Adapted excerpts from *Champion Kep*, by William
> > H. Ogilvie, 1909
>
> Farewell Mickey; rest well boy.
> Thank you for giving us years of joy.
>
> > —Helen Parkin

Contents

Part 2
Honing Your Skills

14 PRACTICE MAKES PERFECT   113

15 FINE-TUNING YOUR BOX WORK   115

16 FINE-TUNING YOUR JUMPING   129

17 PUTTING FINE-TUNED ELEMENTS TOGETHER   141

Foreword

Having attended Jackie Parkin's seminars and successfully used her methods in our own flyball classes for the past two years, it is a great honor for me to write the foreword for her book, which will revolutionize the sport of flyball.

Jackie Parkin has been involved in training dogs for more than fifteen years. She founded and operates Canadian Animal Actors and Casting, a company that provides animals for motion pictures and commercials.

Jackie is accomplished in many aspects of animal training. She has written articles on cat training for *Humane Innovations & Alternatives* (published by Psychologists for the Ethical Treatment of Animals), delivers flyball seminars, has worked in a veterinarian hospital for more than twelve years and is a Northern Borders Flyball Team captain. Jackie's involvement with various other clubs and teams has allowed her to draw on personal experiences to create clear and concise training methods for both experienced and novice teams. She has personally trained nine dogs, of different breeds, that have achieved flyball titles.

Using her keen sense of detail and her understanding of positive animal training techniques, Jackie has written a book that breaks down the sport of flyball into small building blocks—from retrieving the ball to executing a "swimmer's turn" on the box. She describes the basic elements of the game and presents individual training exercises using primary and secondary motivators.

This book not only demonstrates the basics, but provides a clear way to correct and prevent problems. You will learn to develop advanced strategies, such as forming your team lineup, and improving both individual and team performance. Additional tips on traveling and dealing with different breeds and personalities will not only show you how to make a better team, but will also make the competition more fun.

I know you will find this book invaluable in setting reasonable, attainable goals for your own performance training program, and you will use it as a reference manual for making your flyball team more competitive.

We're at the start line. Listen!

Handlers ready? . . .

John Mairs
Tamsu Learning Centre

Preface

Due to the countless questions that I have been asked about flyball, I have become acutely aware of the necessity for a text on this topic. Because training is a continuous learning experience, I can certainly make no claim to absolute knowledge. However, of one thing I am absolutely certain: Flyball should be fun for both dog and handler. This applies not only to playing the game competitively, but also, and most especially, to training for the sport. I believe that everyone has something to give and to gain from one another, and I hope that my experience will be of benefit to you.

Flyball has undergone many changes during its evolution and will undoubtedly continue to do so. Today's standards were unimaginable when flyball was in its infancy. Even the most ambitious of competitors didn't foresee the level of excellence achieved by our canine athletes. I can remember the first time a dog broke six seconds . . . it was thought to be remarkable! Nowadays there are running times of just under four seconds! Training has improved, equipment has improved, and, ultimately, the sport has improved.

I am strongly opposed to dogs becoming "tools of the trade," which, unfortunately, is a trend in many competitive dog sports. A dog's "worth" should never be determined by his flyball performance. After all, a greater portion of his life is spent as your companion. If you judge a dog's worth based on his flyball performance, choose a breed of dog solely for the purpose of flyball (i.e., a breed to which you are not partial and would not normally own), or get rid of a dog because he's not "fast enough" or because he can no longer play flyball due to an injury or illness, the dog has become nothing more than a tool. By the same token, if you breed a dog (or to a dog) based exclusively on his flyball performance with no regard for temperament and/or genetic history, your priorities are misplaced. This is *not* what flyball is all about. You should never use a dog for your own glorification.

Flyball is a sport for all dogs and their people, and there are many levels of competition. Obviously, some dogs and breeds of dogs will be more athletic than others, but my advice is to enjoy this sport with the breed of dog you love.

I should tell you that this is not a book that promotes training through force. The methods of training taught in this text are based on positive reinforcement and respect for the canine student. In her book *A Dog's Life in the Dales* (published by Smith Gryphon Ltd., 1992), Katy Cropper says, "Partnership between a handler and his dog is a sensitive thing, and the weight of responsibility for a successful outcome, at work and play, rests firmly on the handler every time."

In these pages I share with you my theories and methods that have helped me to be successful in the exciting sport of flyball. May you and your pal—any kind of dog—learn to play, improve your game, and compete successfully.

Acknowledgments

I would like to extend my heartfelt thanks to the following people:

To my parents for their undaunting support and encouragement during the writing of this book.

To Marion Brinkman and John Sullivan for their expertise in transferring my rough manuscript to acceptable computer format.

To John Mairs for his enthusiastic endorsement of my training methods.

To Diane McWhinnie, Valerie Baldwin, Sheila Kuja, Clara Theiss, Jessica Catherwood, and all of their dogs for appearing in the photos necessary to this text.

To John Peters for supplying information and charts regarding the electronic lighting system.

To Ron Parkin (my dad), Howard Kadish, and Diane McWhinnie for their time and patience in taking photographs for this book.

To Howard Kadish for drawing the cartoons for this book.

To John Robichaud for drawing the diagrams for this book.

To Pat Morgan and members of the Fur Fun Flyball Team for supplying photographs of their many different breeds of dogs enjoying the sport.

To Helen Parkin (my mum) for proofreading the manuscript for typos!

And, last but not least, to Alpine Publications, without which this book would still be an unfulfilled dream.

Introduction

My first introduction to the sport of flyball was at the 1985 Toronto Sportsman's Show. A small competition was in progress and as I watched, fascinated, I thought, "Mickey would love this!" I went home with a mission—to become involved with flyball.

I called every dog training facility in my area to ask whether or not flyball was a part of their curriculum and was met with one disappointment after another. Finally, a trainer by the name of Ginny Neher approached me and asked if I would be interested in joining a new flyball team that she was forming. And so it was that Mickey-Finn and I became founding members of the Fastlane Flyball Team. Little did I know that I was about to embark on a path that would lead me to the writing of this book.

Since its inception, flyball has become one of the fastest-growing canine sports in North America and, in recent years, has spread to other countries as well. The popularity of the sport can probably be attributed to the fact that it is a sport for all dogs—purebreds and mixed breeds. In fact, the open door to mixed breed dogs was one of the aspects of the sport that first caught my attention. (Mickey-Finn was a Collie/Labrador mix, and my younger dog, Shannon, is a Samoyed mix). Although I was actively involved with obedience training with my dogs, they were not eligible for formal competition. Only purebred dogs are permitted to participate in obedience competition. (There is now an organization called AMBOR that holds obedience competitions for mixed-breed dogs.) Flyball gave me the opportunity to become involved with a recognized canine activity and earn titles for my dog. It was my ticket to entering the dog show world as a serious trainer and competitor.

One of the most amazing things about flyball is that it attracts people from all walks of life. Participants are engineers, truck drivers, homemakers, professional dog trainers, veterinarians, school teachers—you name it—all equals with a common interest. Flyball also attracts people of all ages, from children to senior citizens. At tournaments you may see several generations competing in this sport. Children who are not yet big (or strong) enough to run a dog in competition can often be seen catching stray balls and/or holding on to the backup dogs. However, there are some junior handlers, such as ten-year-old Jessica Catherwood (with my flyball team) running dogs at tournaments and/or flyball demonstrations.

Because flyball is a race, concerns such as tough judge versus easy judge do not exist. A race is a race. Whichever team's anchor dog crosses the finish line first, wins. Plain and simple. This simplicity is probably the single most important factor that has contributed to the popularity of flyball as a spectator sport, because everyone understands a race.

For the competitor, flyball offers the opportunity to participate at many levels. Although there are teams racing in less than eighteen seconds, as well as those that run in the thirty-second range, there is a place in competition for everyone. And all dogs can earn points toward titles. In a tournament, teams are grouped into divisions based on speed, so everyone is competing against their peers. Not only is there a place for the superfast four-second dog, there is also a niche for the eight-second (or slower) dog.

While the uninitiated may think that flyball is a sport requiring little or no "real" training, let me assure you that this is not so. Most flyball dogs are well educated in obedience and many are accomplished agility dogs as well. It is a fallacy that in order to be quick, a dog must be a hyperactive idiot. Those who have been known to comment, "Those dogs may be fast, but they're impossible to live with," have likely not had occasion to live with a top flyball dog. The best flyball performers are also the best trained dogs in the field, not to mention nice house dogs. Aggressiveness is absolutely not tolerated and, in North America, a dog can be banned from competition for up to one year for aggressive behavior. The fact that these dogs function so efficiently and in such harmony is a tribute to the training that they receive.

Even though cash prizes are allowed in flyball competition, they are not offered at most tournaments. The main reason for this concerns the welfare of the dogs. Generally speaking, cash prizes (in any sport) tend to make competition more fierce and have the potential to make the prize more important than the game and, therefore, more important than the dogs that play the game. Finances are another reason that cash prizes are not usually awarded. Most tournaments do not generate enough profit to afford cash prizes, and the majority of sponsors prefer to give product rather than money. The North American Flyball Association (NAFA) has put a limit of five hundred dollars on any cash prizes awarded to any individual or team.

As with all competitive dog sports, most people become involved in flyball because it looks like fun. The degree of competitiveness relates directly to the personality of the dog owner/trainer/team. For some teams, the main goal is to be the best, fastest, highest placed team in the league. Others strive to be "in the ribbons" in the division in which they race. And for some people, the goal is simply to earn points and title dogs. Regardless of the level of competition, I believe that we should all play flyball for fun—for us and for the enjoyment it gives to our dogs. If flyball ceases to be fun, it's time to quit!

Although all breeds of dogs are encouraged in flyball competition, some breeds are naturally more athletic than others. For this reason, it is very important to be realistic and appreciative of your dog's personal capabilities. I am no less thrilled with my Siberian Husky's racing time of 7.05 seconds, than I am with my Border Collie's 4.1-second racing time. To compare the two dogs would be like comparing apples to oranges. Bobby, my Husky, is nine years of age. Just seeing him have fun playing flyball is reward enough for me.

The *ideal* flyball dog is athletic, agile, and a good retriever with lots of stamina. A passion for tennis balls also helps! Herding and sporting breeds are especially talented at flyball, and Border Collies, in particular, have emerged as the premier flyball competitor.

As an aspiring flyball enthusiast with more than one dog, you may be wondering which dog would be the better flyball candidate. The answer to this question is purely subjective, as it relates directly to your personal goals. If you are a highly competitive person, you will want to choose the more athletic, agile, and faster running of your dogs. But remember, there is a niche for *all* dogs in flyball, so why not play with both companions? I feel very strongly that the main reason to engage in any dog sport should be to enjoy your dog and the pleasure that the sport gives to him. I wouldn't dream of denying a dog the joy of playing flyball just because he hasn't the potential to be super fast.

Flyball is currently established and enjoyed on two continents—North America and Europe—and is spreading to new countries continually.

The record times for flyball are as follows: the continental record is
23.56 seconds and is held by KWVH, Hoboken, Belgium; the European
record is 18.01 seconds and is held by the Jets, South Hampton area,
England; and the North American record (and also the World record) is
16.96 seconds, and is held by Instant Replay Gold, Ontario, Canada.
(These statistics are current as of November 1995.) In 1995, approximately 3,700 dogs competed in flyball competition in North America,
and interest continues to grow.

Through flyball, I have had the opportunity to meet many wonderful
and interesting people in both Canada and the United States. Traveling to
out-of-town tournaments is exciting not only for the competition, but also
for the chance to meet good friends. I have made friends in places to
which I might never have traveled, if not for flyball.

Breeds of dogs that have achieved flyball titles in North America. (Current as of September 30, 1995.)

Airedale Terrier	Border Terrier
Alaskan Malamute	Borzoi
American Bulldog	Boston Terrier
American Cocker Spaniel	Bouvier des Flandres
American Eskimo	Boxer
American Staffordshire	Brittany Spaniel
American Water Spaniel	Bulldog
Australian Cattle Dog	Cairn Terrier
Australian Kelpie	Cardigan Welsh Corgi
Australian Shepherd	Catahoula Leopard Dog
Australian Terrier	Cavalier King Charles Spaniel
Beagle	Chesapeake Bay Retriever
Bearded Collie	Curly-Coated Retriever
Bedlington Terrier	Dachshund
Belgian Groenendael	Dalmation
Belgian Malinois	Doberman Pinscher
Belgian Tervuren	English Bull Terrier
Bernese Mountain Dog	English Cocker Spaniel
Bichon Frise	English Pointer
Black and Tan Coonhound	English Setter
Bolognese	English Springer Spaniel
Border Collie	Flat-Coated Retriever

Foxhound
Fox Terrier
German Shepherd Dog
German Shorthaired Pointer
German Wirehaired Pointer
Giant Schnauzer
Golden Retriever
Gordon Setter
Great Dane
Greyhound
Harrier Hound
Irish Setter
Irish Terrier
Irish Water Spaniel
Italian Greyhound
Jack Russell Terrier
Keeshond
Kerry Blue Terrier
Labrador Retriever
Miniature Pinscher
Miniature Poodle
Miniature Schnauzer
Mixed Breed Dogs
Newfoundland
Norwegian Elkhound
Norwich Terrier
Nova Scotia Duck Tolling
    Retriever
Old English Sheepdog
Otter Hound
Papillon
Pembroke Welsh Corgi
Petit Basset Griffon Vendéen
Pharaoh Hound
Pomeranian
Portuguese Water Dog
Pug
Rat Terrier
Rhodesian Ridgeback

Rottweiler
Rough Collie
Saint Bernard
Saluki
Samoyed
Schipperke
Scottish Terrier
Shetland Sheepdog
Shiba Inu
Siberian Husky
Silky Terrier
Smooth Collie
Soft-Coated Wheaton Terrier
Spinoni Italiani
Staffordshire Bull Terrier
Standard Poodle
Standard Schnauzer
Tibetan Terrier
Toy Fox Terrier
Toy Manchester Terrier
Toy Poodle
Vizsla
Weimaraner
Welsh Springer Spaniel
Welsh Terrier
West Highland White Terrier
Whippet
Yorkshire Terrier

Part I

Learning to Play Flyball

1

The Sport of Flyball

Faster than a speeding bullet, more powerful than a locomotive, able to leap hurdles in a single bound—It's a bird! It's a plane! It's a . . . dog? That's right! It's a flyball dog.

Flyball is a relay race in which dogs race over a series of four hurdles to retrieve a tennis ball from a specially designed flyball box. The dog must push a pedal on the front of the box in order to activate a trigger mechanism that releases the ball. When the tennis ball springs out of the box, the dog catches the ball and brings it back over the four jumps to his handler. As he crosses the start/finish line, another dog races past him to repeat the same procedure. It is considered to be a perfect exchange when dogs pass each other "nose to nose" on the start/finish line. Teams of four dogs race against each other for the win.

Flyball originated in California in 1972 and is said to have evolved from scent hurdle racing. In the latter sport, dogs race over a series of four hurdles to retrieve a scented article. The object being retrieved is the main difference between these two sports. In flyball, the dog retrieves a tennis ball and in scent hurdle racing the dog retrieves a dumbbell.

When flyball was first introduced, the ball was flung upward, high into the air, and the dogs would leap up to catch it. Later competitors decided that this was dangerous to the dogs and the game evolved (as all sports do). Allowing a dog to fling himself haplessly into the air can result in all sorts of injuries, including torn cruciate ligaments and injuries to the spine. Over the years, we have learned that even high jumping for Frisbees can be dangerous to our dogs if they don't jump

Flyball Dog Master Brandy, a Corgi owned and
trained by Debbie Wade of Michigan.

and, more importantly, *land* correctly (a task that competition Frisbee dogs are taught to execute properly).

In 1985, the North American Flyball Association (NAFA) was formed by Mike Randall. The intent was to standardize flyball rules so that all enthusiasts would be competing with the same goals. In this way, flyballers could travel to tournaments in different regions, because the rules would be consistent. This, in turn led to the growth of the sport. In 1985, when NAFA was in its infancy, there were only twelve competitive flyball clubs/teams listed. As of October 1995, there were 164 clubs representing 276 teams in the regular classes and 142 teams in the multi-breed classes. The number of teams competing changes continually as new teams are formed. NAFA seeds (or ranks) all teams based on their best racing time achieved in the last three tournaments in which they competed. A seeded team does not have to compete in preliminary play-offs. The seeded teams and their times are published quarterly in *The Finish Line*—a flyball newsletter.

Currently, there are two official associations that govern the sport—NAFA and the British Flyball Association (BFA). Although flyball has indeed spread to continental Europe, an official governing body has not

"Faster than a speeding bullet, more powerful than a locomotive,
able to leap hurdles in a single bound—it's a bird, it's a plane,
it's a ... DOG? That's right! It's a flyball dog!

yet been established. According to the BFA, they are currently the best source of information for Europe.

THE FLYBALL COURSE

Currently, the dog runs a 51-foot course—a total of 102 feet down and back. During this 102-foot run, the dogs will negotiate a total of eight hurdles (four each way) as well as trigger the box and catch the ball. The fastest dogs perform this feat with an average time of 4–4.2 seconds! A very small handful of Border Collies, including Bell's Jade, Besslin's Wee Whisper, and Bell's Kevah, have actually run the flyball course in 3.96 seconds! Can you imagine that? Probably not. Flyball is a sport that has to be seen to be believed.

The flyball course consists of four hurdles and a flyball box. The first hurdle is situated six feet from the start/finish line. The other three hurdles are positioned ten feet apart and the flyball box is placed fifteen feet from the last hurdle. The handler releases the dog to run the

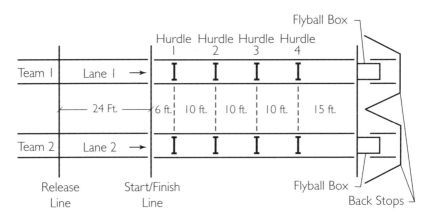

The flyball course is 51 feet—a total of 102 feet down and back.

course from the release line, approximately twenty-four feet behind the start/finish line. As the dog races toward the flyball course, the handler runs behind him and coaches him to "Go, go, go!" Because the rules state that the dog must run the course alone, the handler must not cross

Any breed of dog can compete in the sport of flyball.
Photo by Zuma Press, Inc.

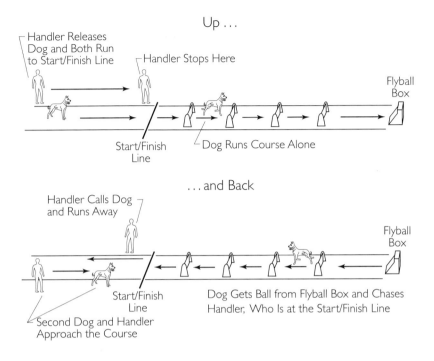

Up ...

Handler Releases
Dog and Both Run
to Start/Finish Line

Handler Stops Here

Flyball
Box

Start/Finish
Line

Dog Runs Course Alone

... and Back

Handler Calls Dog
and Runs Away

Flyball
Box

Start/Finish
Line

Dog Gets Ball from Flyball Box and Chases
Handler, Who Is at the Start/Finish Line

Second Dog and Handler
Approach the Course

Schematic of one run of the flyball course—up to the
flyball box and back to the start/finish line.

the start/finish line. The handler waits behind the line until the dog
reaches the flyball box, and then calls the dog and runs away from the
start/finish line. As the handler runs away, another dog/handler duo
approaches the course. The second dog handler releases the dog from
the release line and, hopefully, the dogs will pass each other nose to
nose at the start/finish mark (a perfect exchange).

This procedure is repeated four times as a team of four individual
dogs run the course. This sequence is called a *heat*. A race typically
consists of three or five heats.

FLYBALL TITLES

A team is timed from the instant that the first dog crosses (i.e., touches with any part of his body—in the air or on the ground) the start/fin-
ish line going onto the flyball course, until the fourth dog crosses the

start/finish line on completion of the course. Titles are awarded to the dogs based on a point system. Each dog that races in a heat will receive a designated number of points according to the cumulative racing time of the four dogs running the course.

In North America, there are currently eight titles of achievement:

- Flyball Dog (FD)
- Flyball Dog Excellent (FDX)
- Flyball Dog Champion (FDCh)
- Flyball Dog Master (FM)
- Flyball Dog Master Excellent (FMX)
- Flyball Dog Master Champion (FMCh)
- The "Onyx" Plaque
- Flyball Dog Grand Champion

Details regarding the number of points needed for each title, are addressed in Chapter 13, Basic Rules of Racing.

FLYBALL TOURNAMENTS

Tournaments are usually hosted by individual flyball teams/clubs that apply for a sanction from the governing body in their country. Sometimes teams will offer nonsanctioned tournaments, but there are no points toward titles awarded at these tourneys, because in order for dogs to earn points/titles, the event has to be sanctioned by the governing body. In North America, approximately seventeen to twenty-five sanctioned flyball tournaments are held per year. New tournaments are continually being added, as teams decide to take on the task of hosting an event. Sometimes a tournament held one year will not be offered the next year because of a loss of venue or for financial reasons. The rental of arenas large enough to host a flyball tournament can be extremely costly and often entry fees alone (collected from teams wishing to race in the tourney) cannot support this expense.

Tournaments have either a "limited entry" or an "unlimited entry." All entries are accepted on a first come/first serve basis. In a limited entry tournament, the host team/club decides on the number of teams that may enter. Multiple entries from an individual team (e.g., Northern Borders A, Northern Borders B, Northern Borders C, etc.) are treated as one entry until after the tournament closing date. At that time, any remaining openings are filled by the second entry for those teams that enter more than one racing team, followed by the third entry from teams that enter more than two teams, and so on until all allowed entries for the tournament are filled. As the sport grows, it is becoming increasingly difficult to secure entries for more than one racing team per flyball club in a limited tournament.

FLYBALL TEAMS

Although some flyball teams are affiliated with obedience schools or obedience clubs, the majority of teams are simply made up of a group of enthusiasts who train and compete together in the sport of flyball. A flyball team can consist of as many or as few people and dogs as the individual group feels able to accommodate. For example, my team—Northern Borders—is currently made up of ten people and twenty-six dogs. Not all dogs on the team can be accommodated at every tournament, however, especially in a limited-entry tournament. Even with four racing teams entered in an unlimited tournament, only twenty-four dogs can compete, because a racing team is allowed a maximum of six dogs each. To accommodate everyone on our Northern Borders team, we would need to enter five racing teams and to do this we would need to have five different height dogs, because each dog entered in a tournament can only be listed on *one racing team.* (The hurdle heights are set to four inches below the wither of the smallest dog in the lineup—to a minimum of eight inches.)

To understand the teams within the team concept, think of the *flyball team* and the *flyball club* as the same entity. Under the umbrella of the flyball team/club, there are groupings of dogs that form *racing teams*, and within the racing teams, there are the *racing lineups*.

A *flyball team* is a group of people and dogs who join together to train and compete in the sport of flyball. The *racing team* is the combination of six dogs grouped together to race in a tournament. The *racing lineup* is the group of four dogs that race in a given heat. Even though six dogs are listed on the racing team, only four dogs race at one time. You can change your racing lineup (using dogs listed on the racing team) between heats.

Under the umbrella of your flyball team, the dogs can be moved from one racing team to another from one tournament to another (e.g.,

RACING TEAMS | RACING LINEUPS

RACING TEAMS	RACING LINEUPS
Northern Borders A:	Ruffian, Casey, Kyle, Davy, Shade, Aisling
Northern Borders B:	Isis, Zac, Kep, Kate, Callie, Forrest
Northern Borders C:	Dickens, Ben, Bess, Murphy, Bonnie, Pip
Northern Borders Multibreed Team:	Julie, Bobby, Orca, Skye, Chelsea, Ceilidgh

*For the teams within a team concept, only four dogs from each
lineup of six may actually race in a given heat.
A race is made up of three or five heats and
dogs may alternate between heats.*

Murphy can run on the A Team at the Caledonia tournament, he can
run on the B Team at the Port Huron tournament, and he can run on the
Multibreed team at the Borden tournament). *But . . .* once a dog is listed
on a racing team at a tournament, he is locked into that particular racing team for the duration of that particular tournament.

Prior to the start of each heat, the team captain is required to give
the racing lineup to the line judge, so that points toward titles can be
awarded to the correct dogs.

When entering a tournament, there is a fee *for each racing team
entered.* For example, if Northern Borders only enters an A Team, the
cost might be $100. If we enter an A Team, a B Team, and a Multibreed
Team, the cost might be $300.

FLYBALL AND TECHNOLOGY

Over the years, modern technology has made it possible for flyball to improve and expand. The development of the electronic lighting system (described in Chapter 23, The Team As a Unit) improved the sport by eliminating human error in timing races and calling infractions at the start/finish line. The Internet has made it possible for flyball enthusiasts all over the world to exchange ideas and chat one on one. And, through the technology of the Internet, the BFA hopes to one day host the Virtual Reality World Flyball Tournament, in which flyball teams from around the world can compete against each other on-line.

Now we can move forward and learn how to play flyball.

2

Flyball Equipment

In order to start playing flyball, you need some basic equipment. The most essential and expensive piece of equipment will be the flyball box. However, if you approach established flyball teams or individuals who make and sell flyball boxes, you may be able to purchase a secondhand box for a lesser cost than if you bought a new one. Of course, if you are fortunate enough to a have a person in your group with a talent for carpentry, he or she could acquire the plans for a flyball box from an established team and build one. The remaining equipment needed to play flyball is easier to come by and the expenses are minimal.

FLYBALL BOX

Although the flyball box has undergone many changes during the evolution of the game, one thing has remained constant—the box must be mechanically, not electrically, activated. Years ago, the arm that propels the ball was positioned on the outside of the flyball box. The ball was thrown upward and the dog would jump up into the air to catch the ball. (Hence the name *flyball*.) Shortly thereafter, the arm was adjusted to project the ball toward the approaching dog in order to allow him to achieve greater accuracy and speed. However, as the dog's speed increased, so too did the incidence of injury. Injuries such as broken teeth, split lips, bloodied gums, and bruising to the head, neck, and shoulder areas were not uncommon. I remember an incident when a dog was seriously wounded when he attempted to jump over the arm as it was projected toward him. My own dog Shannon was the recipient of two injuries—a bloodshot, swollen eye, and a cut and bruised forehead.

Then came the flyball box with the inside arm. Early models featured the pedal on the front of the box, succeeded by the pedal that arced over the top of the box. Following this was the new and improved wide box with the platform-top pedal. Thoughts then turned toward designing a box that would allow the dog to turn faster and gain more immediate propulsion for the run back. A swimmer's turn came to mind and this led to the development of a more upright flyball box. The wedge-style upright box was an early model. Today, we have several similar styles in use.

Many theories were behind the changing trends in flyball boxes. Safety, as well as speed, were the main focus. For example, the arced pedal was supposed to improve speed by providing the dog an easier target (more pedal) and enabling him to position his head closer to the ball for a better catch. But, the box was *narrow*. So, in order to turn faster, the dog had to overshoot the box and skid into a turn for the run-back. As the dogs got faster, this skidding turn became potentially dangerous due to possible strain on the cruciate ligaments, thus the wide box design, which prevents dogs from skidding past the box.

It was then thought that if the dog was to hit the box hard, he would get a better turn. So the hard-to-trigger pedal was designed. But this proved to be a failure. Not only did the design cause the dog to "stick" (pause) at the box, it also placed strain on the dog's elbows and shoulders.

We now know that a hair-trigger system is best for both speed and safety. With the upright box design, we teach the dog to run off the box, instead of slam into it. We've come a long way.

There are a variety of top-notch flyball boxes available today. The pedal is generally one of two styles—the full front of the box and the bottom three-quarters of the box. The latter design is the one that I currently prefer. My reason is as follows: With the slant-front design (full-front pedal), the dog has to reach beyond his feet to catch the ball. Although this is not a great distance, it is enough to waste precious time and, remember, flyball is a race! In addition, this reach beyond the feet causes a rocking action that interferes with a smooth, fast, and efficient turn. (The swimmer doesn't make a turn off a slanted wall!) However, the three-quarter pedal design facilitates a faster turn because the dog does not have to reach for the ball at all and he can run off the box.

The outside arm flyball box.

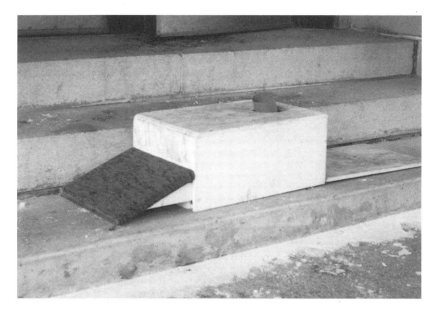

An early model of the inside arm flyball box.

The arc-over pedal box.

This skidding turn became dangerous due to potential strain on the cruciate ligaments.

The slant-front box.

The single-hole flyball box—a popular
style in use today.

The three-hole flyball box.

The depth of the ball when loaded in the box was another design consideration. For a while, the trend was to have the ball protrude slightly from the hole. The reasoning for this was that the ball would have a shorter distance to travel into the dog's mouth, but, alas, this idea backfired. Many dogs started catching the ball in the side of their mouth and/or backing off slightly to wait for the ball. Why? Because when the ball protrudes slightly, the dog already has it in his mouth when the hammer pushes it forward. This results in the ball being slammed into the dog's mouth, which is unpleasant for the dog. He avoids this unpleasantness by backing off slightly and/or flinching his head to one side. Placing the ball flush with the front of the box and providing fast action in the trigger mechanism ultimately puts the ball comfortably in the dog's mouth while still allowing him to execute a superfast turn.

Now we come to the question of holes. How many, placed where, and why? Originally, the hole was always placed in the middle of the box, but the quest for a faster turn revealed that positioning the hole to one side facilitated a quicker rotation, because the dog is already turning when he catches the ball and he has more box available off of which he can push with his back feet. The side hole on a flyball box should not be placed too close to the edge, because this will cause the dog to hit the box with only one foot while the other one remains on the ground to the side of the box. This uneven pressure on the shoulders is not good for the dog. Now, in my opinion, if you are going to use a side hole, you should use a three-holed box. Providing one hole to one side is useful only if all the dogs on your team turn in the same direction. While you can train a dog to turn a certain way, I believe the dog is ultimately faster when he turns to his natural side. To me, forcing a dog to turn right when he wants to turn left is like making a left-handed person write with his right hand. It doesn't make sense.

With a three-holed box, the right-turning dog uses the hole to his right and the left-turning dog uses the hole to his left. If you are the box loader, you load the hole on your left for a right-turning dog and vice versa. The center hole is maintained for the dog that has difficulty with a side hole or that changes the direction of his turn. Although, in the latter case, I would determine on which side the dog is more efficient and train him to turn in that direction only (providing the reason for the change in direction is not due to a change in the dog's leading leg). The center hole is also of benefit to the box loader in the event of a rerun. If the box loader doesn't know which dog was flagged, he or she can load the middle hole and the dog will still be able to effect an efficient turn.

Three separate firing mechanisms are of the utmost importance in the three-holed flyball box. The diameter of the disk-shaped hammer should be the exact same measurement of the hole, so there is no way the dog's foot can be thrust in the hole. The hammers of the unloaded holes must be flush with the front of the box in order to protect the dog from injury.

FLYBALL JUMPS

Flyball jumps can be easily made with plywood. The inside width of the hurdle should be a regulation twenty-four inches, with upright standards that are twenty-four to thirty-six inches in height. I prefer the lower uprights because, when working with a Flexi-lead, there is a lesser chance of knocking down the jumps.

Under current NAFA rules, the minimum jump height is eight inches and the maximum is sixteen inches. For training purposes, I

All parts of a flyball jump can be easily made out of plywood.

suggest a baseboard of only four inches in height, as this is beneficial for starting young dogs of small breeds. You will need four 4-inch baseboards, eight 4-inch boards, eight 2-inch boards, eight 1-inch boards, and eight uprights to complete one full set of flyball jumps. I like to have several extra one-inch boards on hand in order to increase jump

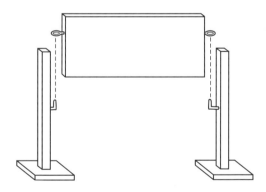

If a dog hits the movable, two-inch top board during training,
the board will move—no broken hurdle, no broken bones.

heights by one-inch increments in training. It is advisable to have two sets of practice jumps so that dogs learn to race against each other without distraction. When setting up two lanes, there should be a distance of no less than ten feet between the lanes.

For the safety of the dogs, breakable boards are recommended and the one-inch boards should always be placed on the top of the hurdle. Better the board should break than the dog's leg!

A unique concept, created by a flyball enthusiast, is the movable, two-inch top board. In this design, the top board bends over if the dog hits it, thus protecting the dog from injury and preventing broken boards. When using this type of flyball jump, pay special attention to how often the dog is hitting the hurdle. If he is knocking almost every hurdle, he is not learning how to clear the proper jump height, because he is running "through" the top two inches of the hurdle. If allowed to continue in this manner, he will be in for a shock when he hits the solid top board at a tournament. This can result in overjumping to avoid hitting the hurdles which, of course, results in a loss of speed.

PIPE INSULATION

Pipe insulation is a terrific piece of equipment that can be used to protect your flyball dog from injury. Cut your pipe insulation (available at any hardware store for a nominal cost) into widths to fit the inside of

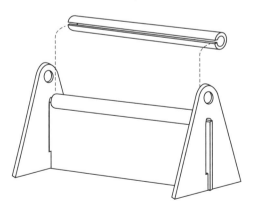

Use pipe insulation to promote safety. By cutting a piece of pipe insulation and placing it on the top board of the hurdle, you can protect your dog from injury during practice runs.

your flyball jumps. Place this padding on the top board of your hurdle to cushion the blow should your dog bang his knees. At the time of this writing, pipe insulation is not allowed in competition in North America, so this will be strictly a safety precaution for your practices.

TENNIS BALLS

Although regulation tennis balls are most often used in flyball, NAFA rules allow for squash balls, racquet balls, and other approved, small balls. Miniature tennis balls are my choice, because they provide the small dog with the same grip (and therefore the same advantage) that the regulation tennis ball gives to medium and large dogs. Also, once covered in saliva, squash and racquet balls become slippery, whereas the tennis ball still has some grip. All balls used in competition must be unpunctured so that all dogs are playing with the same advantages and disadvantages. Any ball that is dropped must be able to bounce and roll.

Always choose the right size ball for your dog. Pictured here are a regulation-size, a medium-size, and a miniature tennis ball. Tennis equipment retailers often have key chains with the miniature balls attached.

It is very important to choose the correct size ball for your dog. Carrying a regulation tennis ball interferes with a small dog's ability to achieve maximum speed, because he has to hold his chin up in order to hang onto the ball. When running, a dog doesn't usually hold his head straight up and tilt his chin back. Therefore, it is wise to start your

small breed with a small ball. If he grows too big for the small ball, you can always switch him to a regulation tennis ball later.

You need two ball buckets for your team. Leave one bucket of tennis balls with the box loader and keep the other bucket at the end of the course to collect used balls. Small buckets, used to keep small balls separate from the rest, are also a good idea. Furthermore, if you have a dog on your team that punctures balls, you should keep a separate bucket or bag in which to collect them. Once punctured, balls cannot be used in competition. They can, however, be retained for training. Mark the punctured balls and use them in practice for the dog that damaged them. In this way, you won't have to keep replacing damaged balls, except for those damaged in competition. I suggest that you put your team initials on all of your tennis balls to identify any balls that might roll away.

Balls can often be purchased through tennis clubs for a nominal fee and are available in excellent condition. Tiny tennis balls are made by the same people who make regular-size tennis balls and are identifiable by the Wilson U.S. Open stamp on each one. These balls are on key chains (you have to remove them from the chain—it's just a little hook/latch—the balls aren't damaged by removal) and can be purchased through sports supply stores. Be sure, however, that the key chain tennis balls you buy are real tennis balls that bounce. There is one key chain ball that is as hard as a rock and you definitely don't want this brand! Remember to look for the Wilson U.S. Open stamp. Medium-size tennis balls are now available, as well, through most pet supply stores. These are suitable for small dogs that are a little too big for the tiny tennis balls.

Motivational toys are excellent secondary motivators that help to make the game fun at both ends of the flyball course.

MOTIVATIONAL TOYS

Motivational toys are used to make the game fun at both ends of the fly-ball course. Use whatever turns your dog on, such as a tug toy, Frisbee, ball on a string, bumper, or food treats.

LEASHES AND COLLARS

You need a retractable leash (such as a Flexi-lead) and a lightweight long line (twenty feet of drapery cord) for distance work, and a six-foot lead for close work. (I suggest you use a leather six-foot leash, because it's a lot easier on your hands than nylon.)

When competing in flyball, dogs are not on leash and therefore need to be controlled by your voice. For this reason, dependency on a

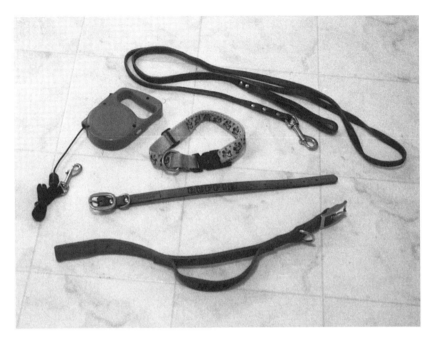

You will require a retractable leash, a six-foot leash,
a flat collar (buckle or snap), and/or a flyball collar.

choke chain or pinch collar for control is not recommended. I train all of my dogs using a flat leather or nylon collar with either a buckle or snap closure.

A flyball collar is a flat collar with a handle sewn on the back. The purpose of the handle is to provide the trainer with an easy-to-grasp area on the collar. Always make sure that the handle is not so big that it allows the dog to put his foot through it. Flyball collars are not generally available through pet supply stores, but can be purchased through obedience schools that offer flyball instruction and also through some dog shows. Existing flyball teams can usually put you in touch with a source for flyball collars.

PRACTICE AREA

As previously stated, the actual flyball course is fifty-one feet in length, which means a suitable practice area should be *at least* eighty

If you practice outdoors, make sure that the ground is level.

feet long. A minimum width of twenty-six feet is necessary for two flyball lanes. Set up each lane six feet from the outside wall, which will leave a regulation ten feet between lanes.

Proper footing is a must for the dog's safety and nonslip rubber matting is the flooring of choice. Carpeting is not suitable, because rug burns to the dog's pads are a certainty. Wood, linoleum, or vinyl flooring; concrete; asphalt; and gravel are also not acceptable. When running on rubber matting, it is important that your dog's feet be kept dry, otherwise they will blister and tear as he skids.

Most tournaments are held indoors on rubber matting, so it is advisable to practice on this same flooring. However, if you must practice outdoors, do so on grass and make sure the ground is level and dry. My first flyball dog, Mickey, pulled a shoulder muscle when he slipped on damp grass.

When preparing to go to an outdoor tournament, be sure to conduct one or two outdoor practices prior to the competition so that your dogs can adjust to the new footing. By the same token, it you are practicing outdoors and are entering an indoor tournament, be sure to train indoors prior to attending.

EQUIPMENT CHECKLIST

- flyball box
- flyball jumps
- pipe insulation
- tennis balls (or other approved balls)
- two ball buckets
- motivational toys
- six-foot leash
- Flexi-lead
- long line (drapery cord)
- flat collar and flyball collar
- practice area

Photo by Zuma Press, Inc.

3

Teaching and Learning

Many people consider training to be a simple case of reprimanding inappropriate behavior, but this is useless if the dog is not instructed in and praised for *correct* behavior. For example, if you want to teach your dog to stay, the most productive method of doing this is to put him in position, give the stay command while standing directly beside him, wait one or two seconds only, praise and reward the dog while he is still in position, and then break off the exercise. Gradually move out in front of the dog and build distance between you, always returning often to praise and reward correct behavior. In this way, the dog comes to understand what *stay* means and gains confidence from the praise he is receiving. This confidence alleviates any stress he may otherwise feel, and enables him to learn and perform the command reliably. The mistake made by many trainers, however, is to put too much distance between dog and handler too soon, and to wait too long before breaking off the exercise. In this situation, stress is created, because the dog seldom gets a chance to be successful and is, therefore, always being reprimanded for breaking the stay. The stay never becomes really reliable (if sufficiently learned at all) and the dog appears anxious when performing the exercise. The rule of thumb when teaching any exercise is to set your dog up for success, not failure. Animals, like people, learn by being successful and by earning praise and rewards. Positive reinforcement creates a healthy attitude and atmosphere for learning (for both the dog and the handler), while negative reinforcement creates stress and anxiety, which interfere with the learning process.

While negative reinforcement does have its place in training, this training tool is widely misused. At dog shows, I witness so many dogs working in fear of punishment, as opposed to working happily and in partnership with their trainers. A flyball dog trained in a negative environment of fear and punishment will never amount to much. He will never reach his full potential, because a dog has to *want* to play flyball in order to be good at it.

Many flyball dogs fail to perform to their full potential, because they are not under proper control. They are not focused. They are just excited. Unfortunately, many owners mistake this unfocused excitement for attitude and drive. They fail to discipline and/or correct their dogs for inappropriate behavior, because they are afraid it will "ruin the dog's attitude." *Rubbish!*

CORRECTION

The underlying problem of ill-trained dogs is not with the *dog,* but with the *handler,* who lacks an understanding of the methods of training and learning. For many people, correction is punishment, but this is a grave misconception. So what is correction? According to *Webster's Dictionary,* to *correct* is to "make right; to remove errors from; to amend." Under *amend* we find, "to free from fault; to make better." If properly implemented, correction should not ruin our dogs' attitudes, but should simply remove errors in execution and improve performance (in other words, make it better).

Correction is not punishment and should not be perceived as such. It should aid in learning, not create fear. A correction is made up of two components: (1) it indicates an error and (2) it indicates the correct response. If a schoolteacher corrects a child's homework simply by putting red X's through the mistake, without correcting those mistakes, the child may not learn why his responses were wrong. Even television game show hosts indicate the correct response to the contestant who has erred. Understanding *why* something is wrong is more important than simply knowing that it is. Understanding what the error is aids in understanding and learning the correct response. And so it is with our dogs.

I usually establish a verbal reprimand to indicate an error at the exact moment that it is made. For example, if my dog is in a sit-stay and he starts to move, I say, "Ah, ah," and then physically put him back in position. But if I were suddenly to rush in at him, roughly haul him back into position, and yell at him, the likelihood of my properly communicating his error would be nil. The negative verbal cue "ah, ah," made at the precise moment he starts to move, indicates to the dog that the error was made at that moment in time. Now timing is crucial! If I wait until my dog is standing on all four feet before I give my verbal reprimand, it is too late to give it. The verbal reprimand has to be given at the first sign of movement. The negative verbal cue is the first part of the effective correction. It indicates the exact point at which the error was made, while the physical action of putting the dog back in position indicates the desired behavior.

Whenever you use or teach a negative verbal cue, it must be followed by some sort of physical negative correction however mild. It is only in this way that the dog can learn the meaning of the verbal "ah, ah," or "no." Your negative physical stimulus does not need to be overly forceful in order to be effective. In fact, it can be quite mild and can merely entail stopping the dog from continuing a certain behavior.

CONDITIONED REINFORCERS

A conditioned reinforcer is also a very useful tool in training your dog. It signals to the dog that he has done the right thing and that a reward is imminent. For example, if I give my dog a treat and praise every time I touch his nose, the action of touching his nose will become a conditioned reinforcer. (The food and praise have to be given within one second of the touch on the nose in order for optimum learning to occur.) Once learned, I can use this action, now a conditioned reinforcer, to indicate to my dog that he is doing the right thing and that I'm pleased with him. The action alone, without the food, becomes a valuable tool. I can now take my dog into the obedience ring and use my conditioned reinforcer in between exercises to signal my pleasure and promise of reward. The dog expects that one of the touches on the nose will be accompanied by a food reward and, therefore, responds eagerly to each touch. Anticipation of reward keeps him striving to achieve that reward. In practice, it is always important to reward your dog randomly to keep him a believer. Your dog has to believe that the reward is imminent. In this way, the dog feels he has some control. He performs *with* you, not *for* you.

A touch on the nose can become a conditioned reinforcer
that signals to the dog that he is doing the right thing.
Photo by H. Kadish

   Your conditioned reinforcer doesn't have to be an action. It can be a word. I like to establish the word *yes* as a conditioned reinforcer for my dogs. This allows me to indicate to my dog, at the precise moment of a breakthrough, that he has done the right thing. It also helps me to guide the dog in a decision-making process toward a desired behavior. For example, when I'm teaching my dog directed jumping, I begin by guiding him with food over the signaled jump, but I can't do this forever. At some point, I have to let him make the choice independently. It is at this point in time that a verbal conditioned reinforcer becomes a valuable tool. I can say yes as an aid if the dog seems unsure. In this instance, I would say yes if the dog moved toward the correct jump, thus reinforcing behavior and giving the dog confidence in his decision.

   We often unknowingly and automatically establish conditioned reinforcers for certain desired or enjoyed behaviors. An obvious example is Frisbee catching. We toss the Frisbee for our dog and the first time he catches it we involuntarily cheer in delight the very instant the catch is made. We then get used to him catching at this level and no longer cheer. The dog, however, has learned to enjoy the cheers of delight and so strives to achieve that response. In a sense, he raises the criteria himself. Now he jumps up and snatches the Frisbee right out of the air and your natural response is to cheer the moment this happens. The dog will strive to repeat this performance in order to get the praise. The timing is perfect! He gets the praise while he is in the air, in the process of catching the Frisbee. It is this exact timing that you have to develop consciously in all other aspects of your dog training.

The use of conditioned reinforcers and positive reinforcement are a means of shaping behavior in our dogs. In flyball, all too often trainers try to get to the end product too fast—missing several steps along the way. These steps are often important opportunities toward making the behavior more consistent. Proper use of correction, conditioned reinforcers, and positive reinforcement will give your dog confidence and understanding of the tasks he is asked to perform. The praise and reward your dog receives will boost his confidence, alleviate stress, and eliminate burnout, all of which are important considerations in the competitive flyball dog.

PERSONAL POTENTIAL

Always remember that dogs, like humans, come with varying levels of intelligence and physical potential. The dog you are training can only perform within his personal potential, no further. It is, therefore, important to recognize your dog's potential at a given time and set realistic goals. To push the dog beyond his potential could ruin him altogether and no dog sport is worth ruining the dog. When you work with your dog within his level of potential, you will often discover a previously unrecognized window for advancement. Why? Because as your dog reaches his potential, a new level of potential often presents itself. For example, let's talk about Kep. Kep was an awkward and uncoordinated youngster. He did everything with *major* puppy mentality and goofiness. I had no aspirations for him as a competitive flyball dog and he was given a spot on our fun team—a low-key, low-pressure team for slower dogs, older dogs, and pups. Then, when he was one and one-half years of age, he suddenly grew into himself, gained control over his great long legs, and made a sudden improvement in his flyball performance. I saw potential that hadn't previously existed! I worked toward that new potential and, at two years of age, Kep became a valu-

Besslin's The One I "Kep."

able member of our championship team. Had I pushed him beyond his physical and mental capabilities as a pup, I probably wouldn't have the flyball dog I have today.

TWO STUDENTS

When thinking of teaching and learning, we must remember that the dog is only as good as his trainer, just as the chain is only as strong as its weakest link. When we train for flyball, we have two students with which to contend . . . dog and handler! Therefore, it is important to encourage and praise not only the dog for good effort, but the handler as well. Keeping the trainer motivated and in a positive frame of mind is just as important as motivating the dog. In fact, it is more important than you might realize, because if the trainer is discouraged he or she will transmit this feeling to the dog (most of the time unconsciously) and the dog will become stressed and confused. The trainer's praise will be insincere no matter how hard she tries to feign enthusiasm. I have seen several promising flyball dogs and their handlers quit due to lack of encouragement in training. I have also seen many promising young dogs ruined (play badly, get injured, have their potential squashed), because the handler hadn't been properly instructed and encouraged. It's not always *what* you say that discourages people, but *how* you say it. If the handler feels discouraged and feels that everyone is down on her, she will take her feelings out on the dog—by being really negative and/or overly forceful in training, by getting angry with the dog, or by pushing the dog too hard in an effort to prove everyone wrong. In this situation, it is not the handler who is to blame for her actions, but the fault of the team or the instructor for not lending support and encouragement to a newcomer to the sport. Be patient with and supportive of your human student. After all, we were all beginners once!

With our human students, the same principles of positive and negative reinforcement apply that apply to our dogs.

> Encouragement = positive reinforcement
> Criticism = negative reinforcement

Constant negativity through criticism makes the handler feel frustrated and inept, and this frustration will undoubtedly be reflected in the dog's behavior. Therefore, it is far better to encourage and praise steps, however small, made in the right direction than to focus criticism only on errors made in the learning process. The desired outcome—a good dog/handler team—is the result of the proper training of both parties.

When we train for flyball, we have two students . . . dog and handler!

LEARNING PLATEAUS

Learning plateaus are often a frustrating and discouraging time for trainers. Just when you think you've made a breakthrough, the dog suddenly regresses. Or, you see continued improvement and then . . . nothing. Don't panic! Just wait it out and work through it, because the learning plateau is a natural part of the learning process.

Regression is also a normal part of learning. It is a sign of awareness. For example, when my team first introduced our dogs to a new and improved flyball box, the dogs were dynamite. They worked the box flawlessly and we were pleased with our new purchase. However, at the second practice, the dogs were not quite so impressive. They slowed down and worked the box almost hesitantly. They *noticed* the change. But, at the third practice, all was well again.

Usually, when training, we can see a steady improvement in our dogs. But sometimes, correct behavior occurs by chance. In the same way that you or I can stumble on a correct answer, so too can a dog. Often, this is the cause of a learning plateau. What happens is that the dog responds to the cues you are giving him, without really being aware of the task at hand. For example, if you guide your dog over a jump using food, a ball, a tug on the leash, or a hand signal in conjunction with a verbal cue, he may simply respond to your body language, not to the task of jumping. Then, when you eliminate all but the verbal cue, the dog is confused. It is at this point in time that the dog becomes aware that your verbal cue plays a role in whether or not he is rewarded. He then focuses all his attention on the cue, instead of on the behavior—jumping. He's not being stupid, or spiteful, or stubborn. As frustrating as this may be, it is just a part of the learning process. Be patient and continue to show and help him. Soon, he will once again offer to jump. When he does, he will have truly "learned" the task at hand and will move toward the next plateau.

4
Basic Control

At seminars and workshops, the biggest training problems I see are lack of basic control and lack of handler focus. Dogs are being expected to play flyball when they barely understand and/or respond to basic commands such as come, sit, stand, stay, and wait. They're being led over a row of four jumps without being taught what *jump* means.

Before being able to control and channel your dog's energy and excitement during a flyball tournament, you must first have him under basic control. Although formal obedience training is not necessary, the fundamentals of obedience are. Your dog must listen and respond well to your commands and, ideally, these lessons should be taught before engaging in flyball training.

Having a good flyball dog requires the same commitment and effort as having a good obedience dog. Success doesn't come by chance; it comes through commitment. Strong basics lead to understanding, enthusiasm, reliability, and problem prevention.

SIT, STAND, AND DOWN

The simple exercises of sit, stand, and down are essential to flyball training. A sit-and-wait is integral to teaching a dog to jump, a stand-and-wait is good for preceding a moving exercise, and a good down is indispensable.

Give the sit command and bait the puppy into a sit while gently tucking his rear into a sit position. Photo by H. Kadish

In order to teach your dog to sit, kneel down and have him stand in front of you. Give the command, "Sit!" and bait him (offer food reward) into a sit while *gently* tucking his rear into a sit position. Praise him quietly and let him have the treat. Maintain the sit position for several seconds (only one to five seconds at first) and then release him by saying, "OK." Be sure to give the command first, followed by the baiting and tucking. When training your dog to do anything, always follow the basic principle of *cue-stimulus-reward*. It is only in this way that the dog can associate the command with the behavior.

As the dog begins to offer to sit in response to the cue (your command to sit), eliminate the stimulus of tucking his behind for him and begin to give the command while you remain standing. As his understanding increases, eliminate the baiting, as well, and simply reward him for correct behavior. Remember that random reinforcement is necessary in order to ensure that the dog is not being bribed to comply with your command.

Once the sit is successfully learned, teach your dog to stand on cue. Kneel down and have him sit in front of you. Give the command, "Stand!" and encourage him to do so by placing one hand on his undercarriage just in front of his hind leg and *gently* raising his rear while

Give the stand command and help the pup by placing one hand on his undercarriage while baiting him forward into a stand position. Photo by H. Kadish

baiting him forward with your other hand. Praise him quietly, give him the tidbit, and maintain the stand for a few seconds. Release him with, "OK," and walk him forward out of the stand. As with the sit, you can eliminate the physical stimulus as the dog begins to understand the cue.

Next on the agenda is the down command. It should be taught from both the sit position and the down position. As with the previous exercises, start by kneeling beside your dog and gradually assume a standing position while giving the cues. While the dog is in a sit position, place one hand on his rear to keep him stationary, give the command, "Down!" and bait him into a down position. When the dog is in a stand position, give your verbal cue and bait him down while *gently* pushing down and back on his shoulders. I must stress the word *gently*. Don't push, shove, or haul your dog into any position, at any time. Once again, eliminate the physical stimulus as the dog begins to understand the verbal cue.

STAY AND WAIT

Although the stay command is taught to the dog while he is in both the sit and down positions, the lesson is conducted in the same manner for

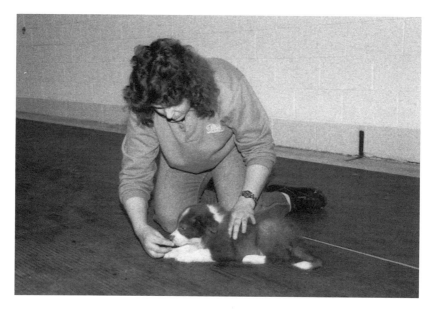

Give your verbal cue and bait the pup into a down position.
Photo by H. Kadish

each. Use a hand signal in conjunction with the verbal cue. Place the palm of your left hand in front of the dog's face. This should be a firm hand movement.

Put your dog in position and, while standing directly beside him, give the command, "Stay!" coupled with the hand signal. Wait one or two seconds only, praise and reward the dog while he is still in position, then break off the exercise with your release command, "OK," and walk forward. Gradually move out in front of your dog and build distance between you, always returning often to praise and reward correct behavior. Don't increase the distance between you too soon and/or wait too long before breaking off the exercise, and always return to your dog before releasing him from the stay. A stay means your dog remains in position until you return to him and give the release command. As your dog becomes adept with his stay, add mild distractions. Remember, don't do too much too soon. Set your dog up for success, not failure.

If your dog breaks the stay before you release him, give a verbal reprimand, such as "ah, ah," the instant he begins to move and then calmly put him back in position. Yelling and/or rushing in at the dog

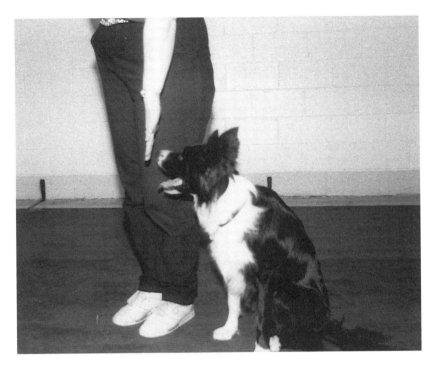

The stay hand signal. Photo by H. Kadish

will frighten him and the lesson will be unproductive. Always remember that temper serves no useful purpose.

A wait is a temporary stay and is used before a moving exercise. This exercise is taught in the same manner as a stay, with two exceptions: (1) the hand signal is a wave in front of the dog's face and (2) you do not always return to your dog before releasing him from a wait. (During the learning stages, return to your dog at least nine out of ten times before releasing him.)

COME

The come command is probably the most important of all the lessons your dog should learn, both for life skills and flyball. Teach the come command by starting with the following exercise. With your dog on a six-foot leash, walk toward a distraction (be sure to keep a loose lead; give it some slack) and, when your dog is not paying attention to you, say, "Come!" followed by a pop straight back on the leash, and run away from your dog and encourage him to chase you. The key to a fast runback in flyball is chase, chase, chase! (Now a "pop" on the leash means exactly that—a quick, unexpected movement immediately followed by a release of tension in the lead. This action should take place in less than one second!) When your dog catches you, give him lots of praise, reward him instantly, and, above all, keep his attention on you.

Once this come exercise is learned, you will move on to longer distance recalls. Put your dog on his long line and have an assistant distract him while you walk a distance away from him. Again, when he is not paying attention to you, say "Come!" pop, and run away. Your dog must come to you directly, with no detours. Keep his attention focused on you for several seconds and always be sure that coming to you is fun, by playing with him when he reaches you.

When the come command is mastered, introduce a sit-in-front. This is taught for the sake of control. When your dog reaches you after responding to the come command, tell him to sit, then take hold of his collar, reward him, and clip on his leash. He must learn that once he comes to you, he must stay with you. In flyball, you don't want your dog to come to you on a runback and then leave to chase other dogs. He must stay with you, out of the way of the other dogs on the team.

When teaching the come command, use a lightweight long line rather than a Flexi-lead, because the retractable leash puts pressure and tension on the collar, and serves as a constant reminder to the dog that he is on the leash. A long line, however, puts zero pressure on the collar, giving the dog a sense of freedom, but allows you to have control.

5

Pretraining and Motivational Games

W hat makes one dog give 110 percent to the race and another dog only give 99 percent? Mental drive. Mental drive is often the difference between a good flyball dog and a great flyball dog. While a good deal of a dog's mental drive is inherited, we can develop and improve mental drive through play. Play is an excellent venue for developing incentive and confidence in a young dog. Pretraining with motivational games should be an integral part of your flyball training program.

CHASE AND HANDLER FOCUS

Chase and handler focus are paramount in the reliable flyball dog and I teach these exercises to my dogs when they are quite young. When I teach the chase, I don't ask my dog to perform a sit-in-front (as in the come exercise), because I want my dog to run to me, all the way, at top speed. I don't want him to be thinking about a nice proper sit. I want his mind to be focused on getting to me ASAP! And I make it worth his while when he *does* catch up to me. How? With a game.

I start my pups with back-and-forth short recalls and I use the dog's name to call him. At this stage, I use a food treat to get my puppy's attention.

Have an assistant hold the pup while you show him the food treat. When you have his attention, back up a few paces and call him to you. Give him lots of lovin' when he reaches you and let him have the food reward. Don't grab him by the collar or manhandle him! Try to keep his attention for several seconds by being animated. You want the pup to stay with you because he wants to, not because he can't escape your grasp! Now, you hold the pup while your assistant calls him. In no time, your puppy will be eagerly responding to his name and you can begin to increase the distance traveled. Back-and-forth recalls are a great way to teach your puppy that responding to his name is *fun!*

In order to build speed and mental drive, I teach my young dogs restrained recalls. In fact, my competitive flyball dogs start every practice with this exercise (over the jumps). To do a restrained recall, have an assistant hold your dog while you show him a food treat or motivational toy. Make sure he wants what you have, then run away and call him. Be certain to give yourself a good head start before calling your dog. Keep running until he catches you. When he does catch up to you . . . praise, praise, praise and play, play, play. Keep the dog's attention focused on you for at least one minute. Make yourself interesting to your dog so that being with you is more fun than chasing dogs.

The purpose of a restrained recall is to encourage and develop the dog's natural instinct to chase, and to teach him to chase one thing only—*you.* This is the reason for giving yourself a head start. If you have what the dog wants and excite him with it, naturally he will want to get to you fast in order to get what he wants. But if you're too close when you call him, he will have no incentive to run fast, because he'll have nowhere to go. Distance between the dog and what he wants gives him the motivation to run. The fact that you run away with what he wants gives him the motivation to run faster, and lots of play and reward when he *does* reach you make running fast worth his while. Play and reward should be whatever makes the dog happy. Most of my dogs run for a tug toy, ball on a string, or another tennis ball. However, my fastest dog runs for a game of roughhouse-and-wrestle, because this is what she thinks is the most fun. Use whatever works best for each individual dog.

Now, we move on to random recalls. In this exercise, put your dog on a long line. When he is milling about, not paying attention to you, call his name and run away. Keep running until he catches you and, as always, play, praise, and reward. If the dog does not respond when you call him by name, give a pop straight back on the leash and then run away—just as you would when teaching the come command.

Show the dog a food treat, motivational toy, or a ball. Make sure he wants what you have, then run away and call him. Photo by H. Kadish

Give the puppy lots of lovin' when he reaches you and let him have the food reward. Don't grab him or manhandle him. Keep his attention by being animated. Photo by H. Kadish

BEAT THE POP

The last part of the flyball game entails your dog running to you and receiving praise and reward. I reinforce this simple behavior by playing short-distance chase games on a six-foot leash. I adapt the random recall exercise into a beat-the-pop game. My goal is to instill a knee-jerk reaction to focus the dog's attention on me the instant he hears his name. The short-distance chase ensures that he will come at me fast, because he won't have time to slow down. (He needs to be educated in a proper, full-speed chase—as in the recall lessons—first.) I often play this cue-pop-chase-wrestle game before going into the ring for a race. Most of the time, my dogs spin around so quickly, they actually beat the pop. This game revs up my dog for the most important part of the game—the runback. What I'm trying to develop is a dog that will not slow down as he approaches me, but will come off the flyball course at full speed and trust me to catch him. I don't want the dog to be afraid to run straight toward me at full speed. I reward this behavior with a tug toy or wrestling game.

WORD CUES

Word cues are all important to getting a dog keyed up for a race and, often, these cues are taught and learned without conscious effort. However, awareness of the cues ensures consistency from and greater understanding by the dog. You can choose whatever word cues you like to rev up your dog, but be consistent.

Whenever I play with a ball with my pups, I refer to it as "the ball." In this way, they associate the object with the word. When I teach them to retrieve an object, I use the cue, "Get it!" and then later I can say, "Get the ball," and my dog knows exactly what I mean.

When I'm teaching restrained recalls, I use the verbal cue "Ready." The dog learns very quickly that *ready* means that action follows. Ready becomes a cue word to rev up my dog for a race. I don't repeat this cue too many times, because if I do, I diminish its impact. Ready means we're ready to go. For example, when running first in a lineup, I position my dog and get him focused by saying things such as, "Where's that ball?" or "Gonna get that ball!" Then, as soon as the judge activates the start lights, I say "Ready," and my dog instantly braces himself for the race. I like the cue word *ready,* because it can be said in a tone of anticipation, which excites the dog.

Go is another cue word that I use to rev up my dogs. When I release a dog for a race, I encourage him with the words "Go, go, go!" This cue is easily learned when doing restrained recalls and basically it means to run away from the person who's saying it. As soon as your dog is released to chase you during a restrained recall exercise, have the holder rev him up from behind by saying, "Go, go, go!"

FUN RETRIEVING

Next on our agenda is our fun retrieving exercise and although your dog may instinctively retrieve, you want to teach him to retrieve with a particular style. The point of the retrieve is to get the object *to* you, not just to get the object. You want to instill a sense of urgency. The dog should retrieve with a sense of purpose, and that purpose should be to get the retrieved object to you as if life itself depended on his speed. Now this doesn't mean that you have to put a lot of pressure on your dog. Indoctrinate this style and sense of purpose into the fun retrieve through motivational learning.

The first thing you need to do is choose a cue for retrieve, such as take it, get it, bring it, or fetch (choose one command only). The second thing is to select something for your dog to retrieve. Choose something that is special to your dog, such as a ball or a toy that he really likes and wants. There is absolutely no point in trying to get him to retrieve something he doesn't want. Remember, he doesn't know the game yet.

To begin the lesson, put your dog on a long line so that he won't be able to take the toy (or ball) and run away with it. Let him drag the line; don't hang on to it. Show the dog his toy and excite him with it. When he is interested, toss the toy a short distance (one or two feet) and give your cue. Praise the dog as soon as he picks up the toy, then call him and run away a few paces. Don't panic if your dog drops the toy when you begin to run. Simply eliminate the run and just back up a few paces until he gets the idea. If the dog drops the toy because he gets excited when you call him, simply calm things down a little. It could be that you are calling him too soon. Be sure that he is committed

Pups will often chase a rolling ball only to abandon it once it stops. Photo by H. Kadish

Praise your dog as soon as he picks up the ball, then call him and run away a few paces.
Photo by H. Kadish

to carrying the toy before you call him. Remember, repetition is the key. Having said that, let me also say, "Quit while you're ahead!" Don't repeat the exercise until the dog is bored. Call it quits while he's still having fun.

As your dog becomes proficient at retrieving, begin to hold his collar as you toss his toy, thereby introducing a slight restraint. In addition, encourage him to come quickly, and slowly increase the distance of your run away (i.e., encourage the chase factor). When he reaches you with the toy, *do not* take it away from him. Instead, play with him, pet him, and tell him what a good dog he is for bringing the toy to you. After several seconds, give an out command (some people say "Give!"), take the toy away, and then immediately give it back. Do this two or three times before throwing the toy for the next retrieve. Slowly increase the distance that the toy is thrown.

If you always take the toy away from your dog, he will learn to play "keep away" with you, as he did with his littermates when they tried to "steal" his toys. This is not the behavior you want to encourage. He'll be much more likely to give up his toy if he thinks he's going to get it back. When you play with him with his toy, let him tug on it and praise him for holding. Use the tug-of-war to introduce a hold command.

Play tug-of-war to teach your dog to hold on to an object.
Photo by Zuma Press, Inc.

Many young dogs will lose interest in a stationary object very quickly. In fact, pups will often chase a rolling ball only to abandon it once it stops. For this reason, begin your fun retrieve with a moving toy. This means that when you toss the toy, release your dog while the toy is still moving (in other words, as you throw). (If you are not using a ball, toss your toy so that it slides across the floor.) When he is confident with this level of moving retrieve, release him when the toy has rolled a few feet away, but is still moving. Next, release him as the toy comes to a stop and, eventually, release him when the toy is at a dead stop. You start the exercise with a moving retrieve and finish with a dead retrieve. But remember, retrieving, even fun retrieving, takes time to learn.

Once the dog understands the concept of the retrieve and is reliable in his response, switch from a toy to a ball, if he's not already using one. Encourage speed and enthusiasm by building up the chase. Call him *as* he picks up the ball and run away. Keep running until he catches you and play with him when he does—just as you did when you taught him the basic chase. Continue to encourage him to hold on to the ball with a little tug-of-war.

When the dog has a dependable retrieve and chase back, introduce a cue-pop-chase into the exercise. Use the beat-the-pop game to instill a sense of urgency. To do this, put your dog on a Flexi-lead and send him on the retrieve. As he picks up the ball, call him, pop straight back on the leash, and run away. However, remember that your basic retrieve and chase must be one hundred percent reliable before you introduce beat-the-pop. A fast recall (instigated by the pop) is the key to a fast retrieve and that's what flyball is all about—a fast retrieve.

Now incorporate a wait into the retrieve exercise. Follow the same pattern of release as you did when going from the moving retrieve to the dead retrieve. Have the dog sit beside you, tell him to wait, toss the ball, and give your cue to retrieve.

THE SECONDARY MOTIVATOR

The next step in developing a superfast retrieve in a flyball dog is to introduce a secondary motivator. When you first taught the chase, you used this tool, remember? Your dog chased you for a tug toy, a ball, or a food reward. We now want to introduce to our retrieve, a trade-off for the secondary motivator. Getting the ball to you becomes the route by which the dog gets an even more favorite toy and/or game.

To teach this trade-off, simply send your dog to fetch the ball, run away from him, and when he catches up to you, offer him the second toy and play with him. Make sure he brings the ball all the way to you before letting him have the second toy. When he is competent at this level, show him the second toy just before he catches you. Don't stop running to show him the toy or he will slow down. If he drops the ball before reaching you, don't let him have the second toy. Instead, send him back for the dropped ball. Don't get mad at him, just redirect him. Little by little, and only when he is one hundred percent competent at a given stage, show him the toy sooner and sooner until, eventually, he sees the secondary motivator clearly as you run away from him. The pattern becomes the following:

1. Throw the ball.
2. Send the dog.
3. Call the dog.
4. Show the second toy.
5. Run away.
6. Make the trade-off.
7. Play with the dog with the second toy.

Now the secondary motivator has to be something the dog wants. If your dog would prefer a Frisbee, don't use a ball on a string just because everyone else does. Different dogs like different things. For example, my dogs Bobby and Shannon like food, Murphy likes to pounce on a second ball, Kep likes a tug toy, Ruffian likes a ball on a string, and Bess and Aisling like to wrestle and roughhouse with me. In the latter case, the game I play with the dogs is the secondary motivator.

CATCH

Catching is an important part of flyball, because the dog has to be able to catch the ball as it comes out of the flyball box. When I teach my dogs to catch, I use the same cue as I do for retrieve, which is, "Get it." I use this command, because my dog already knows what it means. "Get it" means get the ball. It doesn't mean get it after I throw it for you. It simply means get it. Get the ball from the floor, get the ball from my

Ruffian likes a ball on a string.

Kep likes the tug toy.

hand, get the ball from the air, get the ball from the flyball box. It's all the same behavior, so I use the same command. This keeps it nice and simple for the dog and increases his chances of being successful.

In the first step in teaching a dog to catch, I hold the ball in my hand and tell him to get it. In the second step, I move my hand toward the dog as he takes the ball, thus introducing the idea of grabbing a moving ball. Next, I let go of the ball just as he takes it from me. Then, I let it go a little sooner and a little sooner, until I'm actually tossing the ball toward him. If he misses the ball, I retrieve it from the floor before he has a chance to do so. In order to beat me to the ball, he has to catch it. Now, occasionally, I let him beat me anyway, because I don't want him to think he's not allowed to retrieve the ball from the floor if he misses it on the catch. After all, if he misses the ball at the flyball box, he has to pick it up from the floor and continue the course.

When teaching your dog to catch the ball, throw like a flyball box. Don't toss the ball six feet into the air, because fancy ball catching does not necessarily lead to efficient flyball catching. Help your dog to be successful. Aim for his mouth and toss on an angle similar to the one at which the ball is released from the flyball box. Don't throw fastballs at him while he's learning. If your dog catches the ball, but lacks a good solid grip, you can use the tug-of-war game to encourage a hold. Holding the ball is easy for a dog if he has a good grasp and tug-of-war encourages a good grasp.

To encourage a good grasp, use a ball on a string. Toss the ball to the dog and, when he catches it, immediately initiate a game of tug-of-war. If he hasn't got a good grasp on the ball, he will lose the game. The dog will very quickly learn to catch the ball with a good, solid grasp, which ultimately leads to a faster running time. Struggling to hold on to the ball impairs the dog's ability to run and jump with ease.

NO NATURAL RETRIEVE?

Now, occasionally, you will come across a dog with no natural desire to retrieve—like Shannon. Although she has no apparent instinct to retrieve and she does not (*ever*) play fetch on land (strangely enough she *will* bring a stick out of the water), Shannon does play flyball and is a Flyball Dog Champion.

Shannon is living proof that positive training brings results. I didn't raise this dog from puppyhood. I adopted her when she was ten months old and had already been through three other homes. Abused in her first home, neglected in the second, and too much for the third family to handle, Shannon was hyperactive, completely uneducated, and a fear biter. She reminded me of an autistic child, because she was lost in her own world, with little awareness of the reality of life around her.

Positive learning, regardless of the task being taught, develops confidence and trust in even the most timid of dogs. I truly believe that education is the greatest gift you can give an insecure dog. But . . . I digress.

How, then, does one handle the dog with no desire to retrieve? Well, first of all, you need to choose something—anything—that the dog likes. With Shannon, this meant food. I started to *shape* a behavior pattern by introducing my retrieve command ("Get it!") every time I placed her food dish down at mealtime. She was inadvertently learning that "Get it!" meant to approach an object—in this case, her bowl of food. At the same time, I began to teach her some simple parlor tricks, such as shake a paw, and introduced the concept of conditioned reinforcers.

The second stage of the behavior-shaping process involved putting down the food bowl with one treat in it and sending Shannon to get it. Once she had the treat, I would call her back to me and give her another tidbit. I was now shaping a new behavior pattern—go out, get something, and return to me. Any kind of force used with this dog would have brought about a complete shutdown. She was now two years old and learning to retrieve in the Open class of obedience. Gradually, I had to shape certain behavior patterns and then transfer those learned patterns to the task at hand.

Once Shannon understood that "Get it!" was the key to a food reward, I raised the criteria slightly. I replaced the bowl with a rawhide bone—the kind with knots on either end. I chose this particular shape of bone because it resembles an obedience dumbbell, and I chose rawhide because Shannon loves rawhide. I placed the bone a short distance from her and put a small piece of cheese on the bone. Then I sent Shannon to get it. After a few successful cheese retrievals, I eliminated the cheese and told Shannon to get it. Because she expected the cheese to be on the bone, she went to the bone. I praised her and repeated the command. She sniffed at the bone in a search for cheese and then licked the bone where the cheese had been. I immediately said, "Yes!" (conditioned reinforcer), praised her, and gave her a jackpot food reward. Licking at the bone was the first step toward picking it up and I made a big deal over this breakthrough. We did this a few more times before I raised the criteria once again. I now wanted her to pick up the bone before obtaining the food reward. I started to introduce a basic fun retrieve. I moved the bone around with my hand in order to make it interesting and gave my retrieve cue.

Because Shannon had learned to be curious about the bone, a fun retrieve was now possible. At first, she would pick the bone up and drop it right away. But that was okay. I praised and rewarded her for any step, however small, toward an eventual retrieve. Then came the time to raise the criteria once more. If she dropped the bone straight away, I cued her, again, to get it. At first, she was confused, but she knew that the bone had something to do with getting me to give her a food reward. Finally, she picked up the bone, took a couple of steps forward, and tossed it at me. Another breakthrough! Now we were able to move on to a full-fledged fun retrieve.

Although all of this may seem like an arduous and time-consuming task, it really didn't take very long at all. Shannon learned to retrieve and learned to do so happily and reliably. The fact that she was able to learn to retrieve meant that she was able to learn to play flyball, a sport she has enjoyed for the past seven years. (Just as a point of interest, I should tell you that Shannon grew up to be a perfectly normal and well-adjusted dog, despite her rough start in life.)

Flyball Dog Master, Tiller, a Pomeranian owned and trained by Pat Morgan of Michigan, is proof that dogs of all sizes can play flyball.

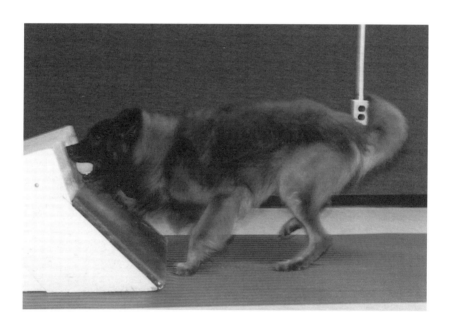

6
Teaching the Box

Operating the flyball box is simply a retrieve in which you raise the criteria slightly for accessing the ball. It's not a difficult transition, if the retrieve is solid. Until the retrieve is one hundred percent reliable, you should not even attempt to introduce the flyball box. A dog with a good retrieve usually learns the box in one session.

When first introducing your dog to the flyball box, test him for noise reaction. Most boxes make a thud when triggered and it's best to know what your dog thinks about that thud before attempting to teach him to trigger the mechanism. Without having the dog too near the box, trigger the pedal on the flyball box once or twice (without loading the ball) to see if the noise bothers him. If it doesn't bother him . . . terrific. If it does, you will have to desensitize him to the sound. Most dogs show no reaction.

If you need to desensitize the dog, the first thing to remember is not to make a fuss over him when he reacts to the sound, because if you do, you are reinforcing that behavior. Don't overreact. Instead, allow him time to get used to the box. Let him watch from a distance as other dogs have fun playing with the device. Wait until he no longer reacts to the box before attempting to teach him its use. Generally speaking, if the dog has a really good, strong retrieve, with a keen sense of focus on the ball (which he should if you've done your pretraining), the flyball box will present no problem.

CREATE INTEREST

The first step toward teaching your dog to use the flyball box is to create interest in it. To do this, show the dog the ball, load the ball into the box, and spring the pedal. The dog should be approximately six feet away and, by this stage of his training, should be well tuned in to the ball and have a solid retrieve. Seeing the ball pop out of the box catches his attention and creates a fascination with this piece of equipment. The second step is to show the dog the ball, load the box, and, when curiosity compels him to approach, spring the pedal so that the ball comes to him. Tell him to get it. Don't wait until he is close enough to be hit by the ball before you trigger the box (the ball travels two feet). Remember, your goal is to get him interested, not to scare him off. The next step is to encourage the dog to run up and retrieve the approaching ball. Be sure to send him with your cue for retrieve so that he knows exactly what you would like him to do.

TEACH THE RUN-ON

When the dog is comfortable with running up to the ball as the box throws it toward him, stop triggering the mechanism for him. From a distance of approximately six feet away from the box, standing next to your dog, cue your dog to retrieve the loaded ball. Then run with him to the box and encourage him to run up and onto the pedal. Have the box loader encourage him to retrieve the ball ("Get it!") as well. This run-on technique teaches the dog from the outset that the box is not a place to stop. Should the dog hesitate to run onto the pedal, simply call him off and start again. Don't let him get the ball without triggering the box and, if he does get the ball, don't correct him for doing so. After all, you did tell him to get the ball.

So how, you may be wondering, will you prevent him from stealing the ball? Simple. If the dog fails to run onto the pedal, have the box loader block the ball with her hand. If the dog manages to steal the ball, it's the box loader's fault for not being quick enough! The more often the dog is allowed to steal the ball without triggering the flyball box, the more often he will attempt to do so. He must learn that the only

If the dog fails to run onto the pedal, the box loader should block the ball with her hand. The more often the dog is allowed to steal the ball without triggering the flyball box, the more often he will attempt to do so. Photo by Ron Parkin

way to get the ball is by putting his feet up onto the pedal. Most dogs learn this very quickly.

The run-on technique is the most enlightening transition for the dog. It is especially useful for Border Collies with a strong eye. Strong-eyed dogs, like Murphy, tend to stalk the box, imagining that they can *will* the ball to eject. It is particularly important that these dogs not be allowed to obsess over the ball as it sits in the box. As I previously mentioned, if the dog hesitates at the box, call him off. Don't let him stand and stare at the ball. As soon as the dog has the ball, call him as you would for a chase or retrieve.

Strong-eyed Border Collies tend to stalk the box, imagining that they can will the ball to eject. It is particularly important that these dogs not be allowed to obsess over the ball as it sits in the box. Photo by H. Kadish

TEACH A FORMAL PUSH

Although the run-on is the procedure I use to teach all of my dogs how to operate the box, and the one that I find most universally effective, there are some dogs that need a little more help. These dogs need to be physically *shown* what to do. In this instance, take the dog up to the flyball box, place his feet on the pedal, and tell him to push. After you've shown him this behavior a few times, tap the pedal and cue him. He will soon make the connection that *push* means delivery of the ball.

USE THE PAW TRICK

If the dog is still having trouble making the connection between pushing the pedal and releasing the ball, you can use the simple trick of shaking a paw to encourage him to put a foot on the pedal. To do this,

The paw trick. Photo by H. Kadish

place your hand in front of the pedal, as if you are going to shake his paw. Then, as he puts out his paw, pull your hand away so that his foot hits the pedal, thereby releasing the ball. Your verbal cue must be whatever you normally say to get your dog to shake his paw.

USE THE COOKIE TRICK

For some dogs that are reticent to push the pedal on the flyball box, a cookie or other dog treat substituted for the ball can provide just the right incentive to get him to push the pedal. As one of my friends once said, "If a laboratory rat can be taught to push a pedal for food, I'm sure I can teach my dog the same trick."

The cookie-in-the-box trick is sometimes good for the dog that obsesses over the ball. Often, he will not obsess over food.

Always be sure to give the command, "Push!" or "Get it!" when sending your dog for the treat, so that he will be able to transfer from a cookie to a ball. Make sure he understands the cue that accompanies the action.

INCREASE THE SEND DISTANCE

Once your dog understands how to retrieve the ball from the flyball box, you can start to increase his send distance. At this time, you can also start to introduce your flyball cue words. Before you send the dog, motivate him with something like, "Gonna get that ball?" This helps to focus him on the box. Then cue him with "Ready" so he knows it's time for action. Finally, cue him with "Go, go, go!" as he runs to the box. Run with him to the box. As soon as he has the ball, call him and run away so that he chases you. Be sure to play with him when he catches you. Remember, *you* provide the incentive to retrieve the ball quickly.

Increase the send distance (the distance the dog runs to the box) by two- to three-foot increments only. Run alongside your dog and use your cue words to help him build speed. In addition, have your box loader call the dog to the box and help motivate him for the runback. When calling the dog to the box, call him by name. Before releasing the dog, have the box loader bounce the ball to get the dog excited, then load the ball and call the dog. Once the dog has the ball and starts to chase the handler, the box loader should motivate the dog with the cue words "Go, go, go!" Occasionally, you will come across a very sensitive dog that will be intimidated by the box loader's verbal cues and, in this case, the box loader should remain silent.

As you increase the distance your dog runs to the box, you may not be able to run the entire length of the course with him (depending, of course, on the breed and/or age of the dog you're training). Whether or not this is the case, begin to back off little by little until the dog is leaving you to retrieve the ball. As he leaves you, run behind him and rev him up by saying, "Go, go, go!" because in a flyball race this is exactly the pattern you will follow. Increase your send distance until the dog is running the full length of the flyball course—to the box and back (no jumps).

CALL OFF

As your dog's skills improve, you can encourage a quick turn off the box. Do this by adjusting the timing of your callback, just as you did when you taught him the basic retrieve.

Up until now, you have been calling your dog once he's secured the ball. Now, call him and run away *as* he takes the ball, thus encouraging a snatch retrieval.

If the dog has trouble catching the ball when you call him with this timing, go back to the previous call time until his skills are more reliable. Sometimes, dogs will miss the ball with an early call, because they try to turn too fast for their current level of competence. How soon you call your dog for the runback varies slightly from dog to dog. Even among my own dogs, I find this diversity. For example, I call Aisling just before she hits the box, Murphy as he triggers the pedal, and Bobby once I'm sure he has the ball.

DON'T POP!

At this stage of your dog's flyball training, use only your voice to encourage a quick turn off the box. If you have done your pretraining, the dog should have a good recall response to his name.

At this stage of training, *do not* pop him off the box. Why? Well, firstly, because you don't know your dog's side yet. The direction of his turn may change as he advances in his training. Aisling was a left-turning dog when she began her flyball career, but as she gained speed, her striding changed and she became a right-turning dog. Secondly, unless your dog has a one hundred percent understanding of the beat-the-pop game, coupled with a tremendous drive for retrieving the ball, he may interpret the pop as a correction for approaching the box. In this instance, you will damage whatever progress you may have made with the flyball box and create problems, such as a slow, hesitant approach. I have seen many dogs react adversely to the pop off the box when it has been introduced too soon. Sensitive and/or submissive dogs are especially vulnerable.

7

Teaching the Jumps

W hen first introducing your dog to the flyball jumps, use only one hurdle set at a low height. While eight inches is suitable for medium and large breeds, I would recommend a jump height of three, four, or six inches for small breeds. I say this because I feel that the small dog should have the same advantage in learning on a low jump height, relative to his size, as the larger dog.

The dog must understand the jump command thoroughly before being expected to execute a row of four obstacles. There is absolutely no point in setting up four hurdles and tunneling him with baby gates, as is sometimes done. This tunnel method of training only teaches the dog to go over the four obstacles when physically prevented (by the baby gates) from going around them. Often, the result is a dog that becomes thoroughly confused and stressed when he is corrected for going around the hurdles—and he will—once the baby gates are removed. He may not go around the jumps right away, but he will surely do so at some point in time, because he doesn't truly understand the jump command. The dog has to make the choice to go over the hurdle on command, without baby gates. Only then does he truly understand the task at hand.

When you *do* use more than one flyball jump, later in the training process, the distance between the hurdles should be a regulation ten feet.

BASIC JUMPING

To start off, place your dog in a sit position in front of the hurdle and tell him to wait. Keep him on leash for now. Walk over the hurdle and turn to face him. Then, bait your dog over the hurdle with a food treat, ball, or toy while giving your jump command ("Over!" "Hup!" or "Jump!"). I use the cue, "Over!" Then, praise, praise, praise, and play, play, play when he does it right. If the dog attempts to come around the jump, say nothing. Simply prevent him from coming around the jump by walking toward him and guiding him back to the starting position. You don't want to discourage him from coming toward you. After all, the runback over the flyball jumps needs to be fast and strong in the end, and your dog must not be apprehensive about coming to you. Scolding the dog for attempting to come to you by going around, instead of over the jump during the learning stages may cause the dog to become unsure about approaching you and/or taking the initiative to attempt the hurdle. It's much the same as correcting a dog for antici-pation on a recall when he's just learning. Anticipation is not a bad thing, but can become a problem through correction. When correction causes stress and confusion, the dog will often continue to repeat the undesired behavior. Be patient. Set your dog up for success.

At this stage, both dog and handler should be very close to the hur-dle. As the dog starts to understand the jump command, put more distance between him and the jump. *You* stay close to the jump, however. As the dog's accuracy increases, you can start to put distance between your-self and the jump. For example, at first, both you and your dog should be only one foot from the hurdle, then your dog should be three feet from the hurdle and you should be one foot away. Then both of you should work from a three-foot distance. Next, the dog should be six feet away and you should be three feet away. Then both of you start at six feet from the hurdle and so on. Until your dog *consistently* takes the jump at one level, you are not ready to move on. Take your time! Work with the dog on the end of your leash and don't worry, compare, or compete with someone else's dog.

When the dog thoroughly understands the jump command and is reliable from a distance of fifteen to twenty feet, you can introduce two hurdles. Start off in the same way as you did for one hurdle—both you and your dog close to the jumps, and slowly increase the distance between you, your dog, and the hurdle. When he's competent at two hur-dles, introduce the third and so on. Begin with the dog on a Flexi-lead

At first, both dog and handler should work close to the hurdle. Photo by H. Kadish

As the dog's accuracy increases, you can begin to build distance from the hurdle—dog first, then handler. Photo by H. Kadish

and when he's proficient you can run him off leash. Eliminate any body language so that your dog is responding only to your cue.

RUN-BYS

Once your dog is consistently taking the row of four jumps, you can start doing run-bys. Again, start with one jump and work up to four. On a run-by, run beside your dog as he executes the hurdle(s). He will get used to you running beside him while completing his jump and will learn to focus ahead. As you run by the jumps, give him his jump command as he approaches each hurdle. It is important for your dog to learn run-bys so that, later, you can run with him and motivate him on the flyball course.

RESTRAINED RECALLS

When your dog's jumping ability is concrete, introduce a restrained recall into the exercise. Have an assistant hold your dog while you show him a motivational object, just as you did when you taught him the basic restrained recall. Run away (alongside the jumps) and call the dog when you reach the second or third jump in the row. Keep running until he catches you and play, play, play when he does. The timing of your call depends largely on the size and speed of your dog. For example, if I call Aisling at the halfway mark, she gets ahead of me and the chase is futile. (*I'm* chasing *her!*) I have to wait until I'm almost at the last jump in order to stay ahead of her. However, I can call Ruffian, a Jack Russell Terrier, sooner.

OFF-ANGLE JUMPING

Now that your dog is a pro at jumping hurdles that are directly in front of him, teach him an off-angle jump. Why? So that he learns to come over the hurdle regardless of his position in relation to it. For example, if the dog misses the ball and it bounces off to the side with said canine in hot pursuit, you want the dog to come back on line and complete the flyball course. If he misses even one jump, he will have to rerun the course at the end of the lineup, which could make the difference between winning and losing the race.

To teach off-angle jumping, we, once again, start with one jump. Place your dog in a sit position, slightly off center to the hurdle. Then go to the opposite side of the hurdle and position *yourself* slightly off center but in a straight line of vision to your dog. Teach the off-angle jump in the same manner as you taught the basic jump. Bait the dog over the hurdle with food, a ball, or a toy, while giving your chosen jump command. This exercise is usually learned quickly if the dog's basic jumping ability is well established. Remember, always build distance between your dog and the hurdle before building distance between yourself and the hurdle.

In this exercise, you will not only build distance, but also the degree to which the dog is off angle. However, do not attempt to increase dis-

Place your dog slightly off center to the hurdle, and position yourself slightly off center and in a straight line of vision to your dog.

tance and degree of angle at the same time. For example, increase distance on the original angle and, when that is understood, then slightly expand the angle. When this new angle is mastered, slightly increase the distance, and so on. Go slow and be sure to work angles on both the left and right sides of the hurdle.

DIRECTED JUMPING

Directed jumping is simply another form of off-angle jumping, except that you use two hurdles and introduce a hand signal. To begin, place two hurdles side by side. Place your dog in a sit position central to the jumps and position yourself centrally on the opposite side. While holding food, a ball, or a toy in one hand, guide the dog over the appropriate jump. (Hold the lure in your right hand if you are baiting the dog over the hurdle on your right and hold the lure in your left hand to bait the dog over the hurdle on your left.) This action becomes your hand signal. Don't forget to cue your dog verbally with the jump command. As the dog begins to grasp the concept of this lesson, you no longer need to guide him over the hurdle. Rather, *signal* to him, coupled with the jump cue. You will still use the food, ball, or toy, but now you will simply hold the reward in the hand giving the signal. In order not to confuse the dog, the transition from baiting to signaling must be gradual. Be sure to work both angles of the hurdle (right and left sides) and, as always, when the dog executes the required task, give him lots and lots of praise.

In the early stage of directed jumping, work close to the hurdle. Expand your distance, dog first, then you, as you did for the previous lessons in jumping. When your dog fully understands the hand signal, begin to enhance the exercise. At this point, and only at this point, increase the distance between the jumps. Commence by separating the jumps by a distance of one foot. Position yourself and your dog as you did when you first taught the directed jump. Signal your dog to jump over one of the hurdles and give your jump cue. If the dog attempts to come through the middle of the two hurdles, say nothing. Simply walk toward him and prevent him from doing so. Return him to his starting position and begin again. You may have to bait him a few times if he is confused. However, if he is well versed in his basics, you shouldn't run into too

To begin directed jumping, place the hurdles side by side and bait the dog over
the desired hurdle using a food treat...

or a ball.

much trouble. Slowly increase the dog's distance from the hurdles, then your distance, and then the distance between the hurdles, and so on.

When your dog fully understands the directed jumping exercise, increase the distance between the jumps and signal the desired hurdle to be taken.

If the dog attempts to come through the middle of the two hurdles, simply walk toward him and prevent him from doing so.

PASSING

When playing flyball, your dog will be required to pass another dog as he goes on and off the course. This is called an *exchange*. We will now prepare the dog for these exchanges by teaching him to pass other dogs without consequence. There are two exercises that I use to teach this lesson.

For the first exercise, you need eight flyball jumps. Set up two rows of hurdles, side by side, and remove the outside posts from each hurdle. With the dog on a six-foot leash, position yourself at one end of the row of jumps. Have another dog/handler team positioned at the other end. Begin by walking the dogs toward each other over the row of jumps. If either dog pays attention to the other, correct him off the course and refocus his attention on you. To do this, call his name, pop straight to the side with the leash (which will take him off course and is the reason why you removed the outside posts), and do a short-distance chase and wrestle. Keep his attention on you for at least one minute. When the dog is able to walk past the other dog without paying him any mind, do this exercise as a run-by. Don't be surprised if he is

When playing flyball, your dog will be required to pass another dog without paying attention to him. To teach him how to do this, begin by walking the dogs toward each other over the side-by-side row of jumps. Photo by H. Kadish

If either dog pays attention to the other, correct him off the course and refocus his attention on you. Photo by H. Kadish

distracted by the other dog. Running canines are a major distraction for one another. If he looks at or attempts to chase or pounce on the other dog, pop him off the course and refocus his attention on you.

In the second exercise, you need only one set of flyball jumps. Put your dog on a Flexi-lead and do chase recalls with him while an experienced dog does restrained recalls over the jumps. Use an experienced dog opposite the novice, so that you only have one dog to worry about keeping focused. The dogs should be traveling in opposite directions. When your dog is one hundred percent focused on you, switch sides with the experienced dog. Now the novice will do restrained recalls while the veteran does chase recalls. This exercise also serves to prepare your dog for running next to another flyball lane.

ADDING THE FUN RETRIEVE

Now that your dog knows how to jump, practically in his sleep, we combine his jumping skills with the fun retrieve. As always, start with only one hurdle. Place the dog in a sit position in front of the jump and tell him to wait. Then toss the ball over the hurdle. Do a run-by with your dog, giving him the jump cue as he approaches the hurdle, followed by the retrieve cue as he lands. As soon as he picks up the ball, do a run-by back past the hurdle, giving your jump cue as the dog approaches the obstacle. When he lands, praise, praise, praise and play, play, play. As he becomes proficient at this exercise, run with him only as far as the jump. Once he is competent at this level, send him by himself to execute the retrieve over the jump.

When this lesson is firmly established, add a chase recall into the exercise. Send your dog out on his fun retrieve and, as soon as he is committed to the jump on the way back, run away. When he has one hundred percent understanding at this level, you can begin your chase recall as he snatches the ball.

Once this behavior is mastered with one hurdle, introduce a second. Begin as you did when starting out with the single obstacle. Run with the dog and slowly wean yourself to the point of sending him alone. When his ability to perform the retrieve over two jumps with a chase is flawless, add the third jump and eventually add the fourth.

DEAD RETRIEVES

Once the dog reaches the point of retrieving over four hurdles, it is necessary to have an assistant put the ball in place. Place the ball on the floor at a distance of fifteen feet from the fourth hurdle (this is equivalent to the position of the flyball box). Have your assistant bounce the ball and call the dog to get his attention, and, as soon as the dog starts to run over the jumps, have your assistant place the ball on the floor for him to retrieve. This exercise is called a *dead retrieve* (because the ball is stationary).

OFF-ANGLE RETRIEVES

An off-angle retrieve is conducted in the same manner as a dead retrieve, only your assistant will place the ball at an angle to the jumps. This is when both your off-angle and directed jumping lessons come into play. You will combine your off-angle handler positioning (at an angle to the jumps, but in a straight line of vision to the dog) with your directed jumping hand signal. When the dog completes the row of jumps and goes off to the side to retrieve the ball, move to the opposite side of the jumps and signal the dog. Be sure to work both sides of the jumps. In a flyball competition, you use this same maneuver to bring your dog back on line in the event that he misses the ball.

Combine your off-angle handler positioning with your directed jumping hand signal to bring your dog back on line following an off-angle retrieve exercise or a bobble at the box during a race.

8
Putting It All Together

Flyball is a behavior chain—a series of actions and behaviors that connect to form one uniform task. Backward chaining is the procedure that we use to develop a competitive edge. Backward chaining is one of the most useful methods in teaching a behavior chain, because each step is reinforced by the previously learned step. I remember learning poetry in school. We were taught the last verse first, then the second to last, and so on. Instead of struggling to remember the end of the poem, it was *easier* to remember, and memorizing it was quicker and more pleasurable.

So how do we backward chain flyball? Simple. Start at the finish! In fact, you have already begun this process without even realizing it! The last part of the flyball game entails your dog running to you and gaining praise and reward (thus the restrained recalls and beat-the-pop exercises). The second-to-last step is the runback over the jumps (i.e., restrained recalls over the jumps). The third-to-last step is the box, which you have already taught. Now that your dog has been thoroughly educated in the elements of the game, you are ready to put the course together.

Start with the connecting link in the flyball behavior chain—the flyball box and one hurdle. Place the hurdle in front of the box and make sure there is a distance of fifteen feet between the two pieces of equipment. Commence by sending your dog to retrieve the ball from the flyball box (do not go over the jump on the way to the box). When he turns off the box, do a run-by over the hurdle, giving your jump cue as you approach. Be sure to play a nice chase-and-reward game once

BACKWARD CHAINING:
Combining the Flyball Box and Jumps

1. box plus one jump

2. box plus two jumps

3. box plus three jumps

4. box plus four jumps

5. one jump plus box plus four jumps

6. two jumps plus box plus four jumps

7. three jumps plus box plus four jumps

8. four jumps plus box plus four jumps

your dog clears the jump. When the dog is competent at negotiating the box and returning over the single hurdle, add a second jump. When he is proficient at returning over two hurdles, add the third and so on. Remember, there should be a ten-foot distance between hurdles, just as there was when you taught the dog to jump.

Once the dog is happily negotiating the box and a four-jump run-back, begin to pattern the jumps on the way down *to* the box. Do this one jump at a time, so that the distance to the box is gradually increased. Have the dog go over one jump, retrieve the ball from the flyball box, and run back over the four jumps. Then have him go over two hurdles, get the ball, and return over four hurdles. Next, have him venture over three jumps, retrieve the ball, and run back over four jumps. Finally, have him run to the box over four hurdles, retrieve the ball from the flyball box, and return over four hurdles. Be certain that the dog is one hundred percent reliable at each step before moving onto the next. Don't expect to complete the flyball course in one or even two sessions. Take your time! Begin each practice session at the level achieved during the previous lesson.

On the way to the box, the jumps are reinforced by the box and the ball. Then, the box and ball are reinforced by the fun of the chase back to you. The chase back to you is reinforced by the game you play (e.g., tug or wrestle) when the dog reaches you. So, you see, each step is rein-

To begin putting it all together, backward chain the flyball course.
Start by having the dog perform the box and a one-jump runback.
Photo by H. Kadish

Progress to one jump, the box, and a four-jump runback,
then two jumps, the box, and a four-jump runback, and so on.

forced by the following step. By teaching the end first, the game gets easier as each step presents itself and the dog gains confidence.

The runback from the box is when very many dogs lose their speed in flyball, and backward chaining can really help this. Be sure to play the chase-and-reward game *every time* the dog comes off the course. Otherwise the chase behavior will extinguish.

Be sure to play the chase-and-reward game every time your dog comes off the course. Photo by H. Kadish

To believe that your dog knows he has to run his top speed in order to gain praise (and to withhold praise for a slightly slower run) is utter nonsense. The dog, if properly trained, is doing his best. He cannot consciously distinguish the difference between a 4.7-second run and a 5-second run. To withhold praise for a 5-second run serves no useful purpose whatsoever. If the dog is trying, he gets the praise. Plain and simple. Otherwise, all the backward chaining in the world won't help, because you'll be eliminating the final and most important behavior in the chain—the reward.

Backward chaining means that you are always going from weakness to strength and this is why it is the key to the competitive edge. For dogs that are struggling to put it all together, or that have trouble keeping their focus, backward chaining can be the point of breakthrough. It was backward chaining, slowly but surely, that turned my Siberian Husky into a reliable flyball dog. If it worked for my dog, it will work for your dog too! Bobby became the first Flyball Dog Champion of his breed.

My Siberian Husky, Bobby.
He is the first Flyball Dog Champion of his breed!

Photo by Zuma Press, Inc.

9

The Running Start

A standard release line is a valuable tool because it gives you a concrete reference from which to release your dog to run the flyball course. It gives you a solid base from which to work and takes the guesswork out of your release timing. (The *release* is the point in time when you release your dog to run the course.) The release line also lends consistency to your exchanges. The release line used by many teams is twenty-four feet from the start line (or thirty feet from the first jump). For most dogs, this is a good distance for a running start. For some dogs, depending on size and length of stride, you may need to take a step forward or backward so that their natural rhythm of stride is not broken nearing the jumps. (Many small dogs use a release distance of twenty feet.) Sometimes a longer legged dog, like Kep, needs to start at twenty-six feet in order to have a comfortable stride into the first jump. From twenty-four feet, Kep has to slow down and take a couple of short strides before going into the first jump. He does this in order to fix his stride for the course. Kep needs the extra two feet to put his natural stride in the correct place, so that his takeoff into the first jump is uninterrupted. If a dog has to adjust his stride at the start line, you defeat the purpose of the running start. The dog's running stride into the first and subsequent jumps should be smooth and uninterrupted.

The idea behind the running start is that the dog should already be running at full speed when he hits the course. Trying to gain speed and jump at the same time is very difficult for a dog. With a running start, he should have lots of momentum to sail over the jumps.

HOW TO TEACH A RUNNING START

When training rookie dogs to do a running start, you need to work your way back incrementally to the release line. Many young dogs will go *around* the jumps when started from too far back. This is mainly due to inexperience. Teach your dog the running start without doing the whole flyball course. The excitement of seeing the flyball box in place is usually enough to cause a "green" dog to go around the jumps. So, initially, just do the row of jumps alone. Remember, set your dog up for success!

Start close to the first jump, at a six-foot distance perhaps, and when your dog is *consistent* in taking the row of jumps from this distance, start moving back one or two feet at a time. Some dogs may be able to move back in larger increments, but you have to know your dog well in order to make that decision. If your dog is doing well and then goes around the jumps when you move back, it may be that you have increased the distance from the first jump too far or too soon (or both). Don't expect to reach the twenty-four-foot mark in one or even two practices.

Even if your dog picks up on the new release distance right off the bat, the behavior has not been learned based on the proper training. I have seen many dogs regress due to owners, trainers, and teams assuming that the dog understands something that he has just done by chance or has put together too quickly.

When initially teaching your dog to do a running start, don't worry about speed. The lesson, at this point, is to make the dog understand that he is to take the first jump regardless of the distance from which he is released. Help him out. Run up to the start line with him, telling him, "Over!" (or whatever your jump cue is) as you approach the jumps. Make it fun for your dog and set him up for success. If he only does one out of five runs correctly, he doesn't know what he's doing. Go back to square one. Show him, encourage him, make sure he understands. Don't increase the release distance until he is one hundred percent accurate at the distance at which you are currently working.

After your dog is doing a running start correctly and consistently, *then* you can start pushing for speed. After all, the whole point of the running start is to enhance speed! Use your cue to rev up the dog and then, as you release him, run behind him, coaching him and saying "Go, go, go!" Another exercise designed to enhance speed is to have someone

The running start ensures that the dog is already running at full speed when he begins the flyball course. Photo by H. Kadish

else hold your dog at the release line and give him the ready cue, while you go halfway down the course and call him. Your assistant coaches him from the release line and you coach him from the sidelines and run with him. Have another assistant throw a ball for the dog at the other end of the row of jumps in order to keep him focused ahead as he passes by you. (You won't be able to outrun your dog!)

The value of teaching your dog the go cue is that when the course is put together, your box loader can use this same cue to help rev up the dog for the runback. And don't worry. Your dog will know the difference between go and no! Your intonation should be totally different for each of these commands. *Go* induces excitement. *No* is a reprimand.

NEW TANK SYNDROME

Now that the running start is learned, *never* release your dog from a closer distance, unless, of course, your dog has a memory lapse! This happened to me when Bess went to her first tournament. The excitement of the trip to the tourney, coupled with the excitement of the other dogs at the tourney, created a new tank syndrome reaction in Bess. (*New tank syndrome* is a term used in dolphin training. When dolphins are moved to a new tank, previously learned behaviors appear to be forgotten until the animals adjust to their new environment.) Bess went around all the jumps and appeared to have no concept of the game whatsoever. In this instance, I moved right up to the start line and released her with the over command. I gave the command firmly, so that she would take me seriously (a tactic to bring her back down to earth), but calmly, so as not to rev her up. A mistake made by many handlers in a situation such as this is to give their commands frantically, thus revving up the dog even more. In this kind of situation, the dog needs to be calmed. Forget about speed. Speed is no good if the dog goes around the jumps. For Bess and I, the trick was to go back to basics right then and there. Start up close, give her the over command, and have the box loader give her this command as well. After a few successful runs in this manner, I gradually started moving back toward my desired release position, still using only the over command. Toward the end of the tournament, Bess was running from the proper release distance and I was using word cues to rev her up. The key to getting her back into the game was to provide her with calm and con-

A strong running start is crucial to ensuring a faster race time. Your dog should be running at full speed when he reaches the course. Photo by Zuma Press, Inc.

10
Teaching Exchanges

Good exchanges can mean the difference between winning and losing a race, and in this chapter we concentrate on the teaching and tightening of our exchanges.

As stated in the previous chapter, once the running start is learned, your dog should *always* be released from that release distance. Exchanges are not learned by moving your dog closer to the jumps. Exchanges are learned by changing the *timing* of the release. The dog doesn't change anything. You do.

Just as with any aspect of this sport, exchanges are learned gradually. At first, no real exchange takes place. Have a dog come off the course and just run by you and your dog. Then, release your dog. In this way, your dog is in a controlled situation. He's learning that it's no big deal for another dog to run by him and he's also learning that the dog coming off the course is not a threat. Similarly, the dog coming off the course is learning not to be intimidated by the dog going on. The dog coming off the course yields (to the right) to the dog going on. Why? Because the dog coming off the course is at the end of his run and, if he slows a bit to yield (and most dogs don't), it is less detrimental to your team time than it is to have the dog going onto the course reduce the speed of his approach. The dog going onto the course is only at the beginning of his run and he needs a good straight run-on to execute effectively the row of four jumps at optimum speed. If he has to swerve to the right to avoid the dog coming off the course, it

interrupts his running start. Now, some dogs will veer to the right anyway, just because they see another dog coming toward them. Often at
tournaments, you will see a coach positioned near the start line to serve
as a "post" to block the swerve.

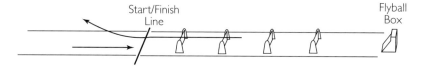

*In a correct exchange pattern, the dog coming off the course yields
to the dog going on. The dog going onto the course needs a good straight run
to execute the row of four jumps effectively at optimum speed.
Position a coach at the start/finish line if needed.*

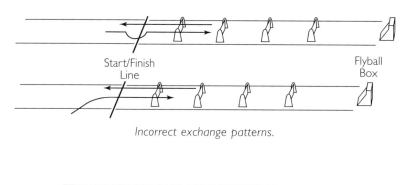

Incorrect exchange patterns.

CONTROLLED EXERCISES

In a controlled exercise of loose, zero exchanges, you can eliminate the
inclination toward problem behaviors (e.g., pouncing on, grabbing at,
or chasing other dogs) *before* they actually become problem behaviors.
Some dogs, when coming off the course, will focus their attention on
the dog preparing to run onto the course (or vice versa). They become
possessive of their tennis ball or keen on the chase. As a result, they
run at, pounce on, and/or grab at the other dog. If these problems occur
during a close exchange, you could have two injured dogs. The potential for a dogfight is very high. Even if no fight ensues, the victimized
dog could become emotionally affected by the experience. A case in

point is Murphy. I had no problems with Murphy running in any position and he had no problems with tight exchanges, until a dog coming off the course grabbed him as he went onto the course. A mouthful of brown hair confirmed that contact had indeed been made. The result? Murphy would not cross behind another dog. He would avoid the dog coming off the course at all costs, even if it meant going around the jumps. And this was *not* a green dog. He was already a Flyball Dog Champion and had been racing for some time when this incident occurred. Murphy had to be moved to the start position for quite a few months and at the same time he underwent retraining for exchanges. Fortunately, time and training helped him to forget this negative experience and he now runs in any position required of him.

LEARNING BY CHANCE

In my opinion, the dog that grabbed Murphy had never been properly trained to do exchanges. This dog probably learned by chance and had—by chance—never actually managed to grab another dog. When corrections for aggressive behavior only take place after the act is completed, it is too late. The inclination toward aggressive behavior has to be recognized and dealt with at an early point in the dog's training. It cannot be allowed to evolve into a problem behavior. (Not all dogs that behave in this way are innately aggressive dogs, but extreme excitement can become almost a hysteria that causes dogs to revert to aggressive behavior.) This is why I emphasize, so strongly, that you teach exchanges gradually and in controlled situations.

COMING OFF THE COURSE

In the case of a dog coming off the course, start like this. If he is easily distracted, run him on a Flexi-lead. Go with him halfway down the course, so that he can reach the box while on the lead. Once he's got the ball, run back as you would if he were off leash. If he shows *any* inclination toward running at the dog waiting to go onto the course, or if he focuses his attention on anything other than you and/or your moti-vational toy (if you're using one), give a verbal negative cue followed instantly (within one second for optimum learning) by a firm collar correction. Don't be wimpy about it. The correction should turn the dog's attention back in your direction, after which you *immediately* focus your dog on *you,* and play with him and praise him for his atten-tion to you. Don't let him end the attention game. It ends when you say so. *You* call the shots. The emphasis on the runback has to be on *you.*

If you can't get ahead of your dog on the runback, have an assis-tant operate the Flexi-lead for you. Use your voice to focus your dog's attention on you, because the collar correction, while distracting your dog's attention away from the other dog, will likely not be positioned such as to direct his attention on you. (The collar correction will direct his attention to the person holding the leash.) Even if your dog responds to your verbal reprimand, you *must* give the collar correction, otherwise he will learn to ignore your negative verbal command.

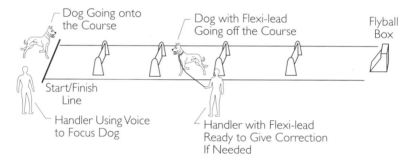

To teach an exchange to a dog with a short attention span, have him run the course on leash so that you can refocus his attention immediately (by giving a pop on the leash) when his attention wanders.

Now you may be asking yourself, doesn't the attention game with praise, etc., just reward the dog for inappropriate behavior? No, it does not. Remember the two-part correction? Pinpoint the error and indicate the desired behavior. The verbal negative, followed immediately by the firm collar correction indicates the error to the dog. The immediate refocusing of the dog's attention to you via the attention game indicates the desired behavior. If you give the correction and then continue to rep-rimand the dog, he will not learn to focus attention on you, but to avoid you. Thus the lesson, focus attention on me, is lost. The only time you would eliminate the attention game and continue to reprimand your dog is if he actually manages to attack or injure another dog. Mind you, you should see the intent *before* it goes that far!

Until your dog can consistently run back without paying any mind to the dog waiting at the twenty-four-foot release line, you are not ready to have the timing of the other dog's release changed.

GOING ONTO THE COURSE

In the case of a dog going onto the course, set your dog up at the twenty-four-foot release line (put him on a Flexi-lead at first) and, when the dog coming off the course passes you, release your dog. If your dog tries to run back after the dog that just came off, a collar correction is necessary. It is often beneficial for your box loader to call to your dog in order to help keep him focused on the course. If the dog shows *any* inclination toward interest in the dog coming off the course, correct him and refocus his attention to the course. *Don't release him unless he is focused* and don't let him turn his head to watch the other dog go by. This could be the beginning of a chasing or grabbing problem. Nip it in the bud now!

One way to discourage a dog from watching another dog go by is to use your left hand as a blinker, if you are running in the right lane. (Use your right hand if you are running in the left lane.) This is how I trained my young Border Collie, Aisling. Aisling was very distracted by movement of any kind. Consequently, dogs running past her were of enormous interest. I set her up to run the course and gave her the ready and gonna-get-that ball word cues. I focused her on the course and had the box loader and an assistant positioned at the first jump call to her. I kept my left hand along the left side of her face to act as a blinker, and if she showed any inclination toward glancing to her left, I gave a verbal "ah, ah" and tapped her muzzle as a correction. I praised and cued her as soon as her eyes were straight ahead. Timing is of the utmost importance. Watch your dog carefully. If his eyes glance to the left, tap his muzzle. Don't wait for his whole head to turn, because it's too late by then. The more often a dog performs an undesirable behavior, the longer it will take you to eliminate that behavior.

Do not change your release time until your dog is consistently focused on the course as other dogs pass by. Your program of gradually teaching and tightening exchanges is as follows: (The dog at the twenty-four-foot release line is Dog A, and the dog coming off the course is

*A good way to discourage your dog from watching another dog
pass by is to use your hand as a blinker.* Photo by H. Kadish

Dog B. Make marks, in one-foot increments from the start line to the
twenty-four-foot release line [more if necessary].)

1. Release Dog A as Dog B passes you.
2. Release Dog A as Dog B reaches the twenty-foot mark.
3. Release Dog A as Dog B reaches the sixteen-foot mark.
4. Release Dog A as Dog B reaches the ten-foot mark.
5. Release Dog A as Dog B reaches the six-foot mark.
6. Release Dog A as Dog B reaches the start/finish line.
7. Release Dog A as Dog B takes the last jump.
8. Release Dog A as Dog B lands from the second-to-last
   jump.
9. Release Dog A as Dog B *takes* the second-to-last jump.
10. Release Dog A as Dog B lands between the middle two
    jumps.

Depending on how fast your dogs are running, you may have to
release Dog A as Dog B takes the third-to-last jump. However, step
number 10 is the correct release timing for most dogs to get a nice,
clean, tight exchange. You may have to make slight adjustments in

release times based on the dogs you are running. For example, if the dog going onto the course is noticeably faster than the dog coming off (or vice versa), you will either have to change your release time or change your release position. Once you are comfortable with a certain timing, it is sometimes easier to change your position. Make sure, however, that this new release position doesn't interfere with your dog's running start. I release Kep from twenty-six feet, because he is very tall and very fast on the release. However, twenty-six feet is also his best release position.

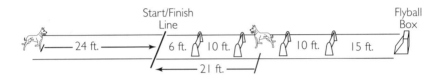

Time your release so that there is a nose-to-nose exchange at the start/finish line. In this example, the dog going onto the course is released at a greater distance from the line than the dog coming off.

Photo by Zuma Press, Inc.

11

Increasing the Jump Height

I have found that the trick to achieving a dog's optimum speed on higher hurdles is to simply take my time in getting there. Far too many young dogs are suddenly bumped up to higher jumps because their owners/handlers want to compete ASAP and feel that the dog is physically capable of executing the higher hurdle. But, physical capability is only part of the game. Just because I'm physically *capable* of walking ten miles, doesn't mean that I should do so without gradually working up to that distance. It is no different for our dogs. They should be worked gradually to an increased jump height.

When you increase jump heights too much or too soon (or both), you make the game difficult for the dog. He still plays, because he wants to please you, but what was once lots of fun is now a struggle. By raising the jump height too much or too soon, you run the risk of dampening your dog's motivation and/or enthusiasm for the game. You also run the risk of diminishing the dog's confidence, creating confusion in the dog, and possibly introducing an overjumping problem as well. Mental drive, enthusiasm, and mental capability are what make the difference between a good flyball dog and a great flyball dog.

START LOW

Regardless of the age, size, or breed of dog that I'm training, I always start off with a low jump height—eight inches for medium and large dogs, and four to six inches for smaller dogs (and/or young pups). I want to make learning as easy and successful as possible for the dog.

I increase the jump height after the dog has learned the whole game. With the introduction of each new jump height, I take away the box and do lots of restrained recalls, always motivating and encouraging my dog. When he is comfortable with the new jump height, I start pushing for speed. When I feel that he's giving me all he's got on the restrained recalls, I introduce the box.

I run my dog at each new jump height until I attain his full speed on that height. When I feel that he is consistently giving me his full speed on a particular height, then, and only then, do I increase the jump height. For example, Aisling runs 4.1 seconds over eight-inch jumps. Therefore, when I move her to a ten-inch jump height, I strive to achieve that same optimum speed, or as close to it as possible, before I increase the jump height to twelve inches.

I make sure that my dog is not overjumping, and is strong and confident during his restrained recalls at each new height before I put the box in place. I want the hurdles to become second nature to him and I want him to be comfortable with the new height before running the entire course at this new height. The sight of the box elicits great excitement in the dogs and sometimes makes them forget that they are on a new jump height. I want to be sure that my dog is sound enough, with the new height, so as not to flatten out too much and bash his knees on the hurdles. I usually give my dog a low-key run of the course the first time out at a new jump height, which is easier said than done!

AVOID OVERJUMPING

If you raise the hurdles suddenly and/or in too large an increment, the dog will often start to arc too high, because he sees a higher wall to clear. By overjumping, he loses speed. I find it far more difficult to teach a dog to flatten out and regain speed, than to make sure he doesn't overjump in the first place. When going from a higher hurdle to a lower one (i.e., you get a new height dog), it takes quite some time before you attain the maximum benefit of this new lower jump height, because your dog has to learn to flatten out and fully utilize the low hurdle. They have to think *run* and not *jump*. A good exercise to use to reintroduce this running-versus-jumping style is to take away the flyball jumps completely and run the dog on a flat surface. Release the dog from the same mark as you would if racing the entire course and be sure to run the same runback distance as you would in a real race. Without the jumps with which to contend, the dog will learn to *run* the course. Once this running frame of mind is established, reintroduce the low jumps.

SLOWLY INCREASE THE JUMP HEIGHT

I increase my larger dogs' jump height as follows: eight inches, ten inches, twelve inches, thirteen inches, and fourteen inches. (Sixteen inches is currently the maximum jump height as set by NAFA. If it's necessary to jump sixteen inches, increase your jump height one inch at a time.) Once past the twelve-inch mark, I have found that every single inch makes a difference to a dog. That is why I raise the jumps by only one inch at a time at this point. Fourteen inches is another crucial rung on the ladder. Jumping higher than fourteen inches really affects speed, and the jump from fourteen to fifteen inches and from fifteen to sixteen inches is a real killer for many dogs.

My smaller dogs are started at a four-inch jump height and progress to six inches, then eight inches, nine inches, ten inches, eleven inches, and twelve inches.

Although I start all of my dogs at a low jump height, occasionally their size decrees how soon they make the first step up in jump height. Sometimes a larger, longer legged dog will be hindered by the lower hurdles. Why? Because their natural length of stride when running full tilt is greater than the required ten-foot stride of the course. In this instance, they must slow down in order not to trip over the flyball jumps. An example of this is seen in Kep. Kep is twenty-four inches at the withers and very leggy. As he gained speed on eight inches, he started to bang his front legs as he took the jumps. Then his speed diminished and he no longer tripped over the hurdles. I moved him to a ten-inch jump height and the problem was resolved. However, when he finally grew into himself, his speed enhanced and ten inches held him back. Now, at three and one-half years of age, twelve inches is the lowest height at which Kep can jump before losing speed.

Through trial and error (and the training of nine flyball dogs of my own!), I have learned that the key to attaining and maintaining peak performance is to increase jump heights by small increments and to work to achieve the dog's optimum speed at each step up in height. It may take a little longer before you get a chance to compete, especially if your team doesn't have a small dog, but it's well worth the extra time, because the training pays off! Aisling was almost two years old by the time I had her worked up to fourteen inches. But at her first tournament, as a member of our A team, she ran the course in 4.31 seconds!

The author with Aisling. Photo by R. Parkin

12
Resolving Common Problems

Most undesirable behaviors can be avoided with proper training. Many of the problems I see in flyball dogs are the result of poor and/or improper canine education. This is not to say that a well-trained dog will never make a mistake; that is unrealistic. However, most problem behaviors in flyball dogs are recurrent and this indicates a lack of understanding somewhere in the behavior chain.

Pretraining and motivational games are critical to flyball training. Even problems associated with a dog's innate personality (e.g., insecurity) can be alleviated through a step-by-step, positive, and fun approach to learning. The biggest obstacle faced by a flyball dog in training is his trainer's lack of patience. Everyone wants to play flyball tomorrow. Well folks, there are lots of tomorrows! Your dog has his whole life to play flyball. Don't rush him.

If I take a wee pup, of eight or nine weeks of age, and start conditioning him to play flyball through pretraining and motivational games, I put a full year of training (on average) into that dog before entering him in a competition. If I start with a dog that already knows how to jump and retrieve, I still do my pretraining lessons and motivational games, and put in an average of four to six months of training time. By taking the time to evaluate and establish (or reestablish) the basics, you can avoid a lot of potential problems.

DOG CHASING

Basically, dog chasing is due to a lack of handler focus and control. As a breeder of Border Collies (a breed obsessed with controlling movement), I can relate to dog chasing. It is a common problem if the basics aren't strongly instilled. Handler focus is what is needed. The dog has to learn that being with you is more fun than chasing another dog.

As with all problem behaviors, you cannot fix a dog-chasing problem while running the complete flyball course. Deal with dog chasing on its own.

Put your dog on a six-foot leash and allow him to observe another dog running the flyball course or playing ball (anything that will incite him into a chase frame of mind). When he "thinks" about chasing the other dog (you can tell by the look in his eye!), do a pop-chase-play without calling his name. Refocus his attention on you. Play with him. Do whatever it takes, without hanging on to his collar, to keep his attention on you for at least one minute. If he breaks off the game with you, immediately do a pop-chase-play. The attention game ends when *you* say so and not one second sooner. If the dog breaks the game off just as you were about to do so . . . guess what? . . . the game's not over. You have to regain his attention and *then* end the exercise.

There's absolutely no point in correcting a dog for chasing if you're not prepared to channel that energy somewhere else. You can't change the dog's emotion and/or instinct; you can only teach him how to deal with it. Teach him that whenever he feels the urge to chase another dog, he can exhaust that emotion in a game with you or on a toy. For example, Ruffian, a Jack Russell Terrier, has a very strong prey drive, an instinct that often expresses itself in dog chasing. With this in mind, Ruffie was taught very early to channel his prey drive into his tug toy. In this way, his natural instincts are used to my best advantage, because he runs to catch his tug toy. The game of tug is his secondary motivator. Once established, the new behavior (focus on the handler) totally replaces the urge to chase. If your dog has a dog-chasing problem, go back to basics.

Now the one thing that greatly contributes to dog chasing, and even creates a problem in certain dogs, is the practice of tying up young dogs where they can watch other dogs run and play. In effect, you are creating a restrained situation in which the dog runs back and forth on the end of his leash and barks incessantly. He is restrained by his leash. This restraint creates a terrible frustration and when the dog is freed, he not only chases, but grabs at other dogs. *Never* tie your novice dog where he can watch a flyball practice! If you are not training him, put him away! (Don't let him sit in a kennel and watch either. This is just as harmful.)

LACKING FOCUS AND DRIVE

Lack of focus and drive are, once again, part and parcel of a breakdown in your flyball behavior chain. Go back to your pretraining and motivational games, and work on your restrained recalls with a secondary motivator if this happens. When these exercises are well established, you need to work on your retrieve and chase. And finally, you need to backward chain the full course, just as you did when you first put it all together.

DROPPING THE BALL

There are three main reasons that a dog drops the ball. The first is that he may not have a good grip on the ball. In this instance, go back to basics—play catch with the ball on a string and use the tug-of-war game to encourage a tight grip and a better hold (see Chapter 5).

The second reason a dog drops the ball is often anticipation over the secondary motivator. Go back to your basic training and reintroduce the secondary motivator as described in Chapter 5. Remember, don't do this retraining on the flyball course. Work on the problem behavior separately.

The third reason a dog drops the ball is because he has not learned to retrieve properly. A proper retrieve means the object must be brought all the way to the handler. Once again, go back to your basic training.

BOBBLING AT THE BOX

Bobbling is when a dog drops or misses the ball at the box. Assuming that the dog has a good catch and has not learned the flyball course before being proficient with the box, bobbling is often the result of the box itself.

If the trigger action on the pedal is too fast, the ball will be ejected too quickly for the dog's level of speed and experience, and he will execute a poor catch. If the trigger action is too slow, the dog may be turning too fast for the ball to be positioned correctly for a good catch. He will either miss the catch or pause at the box to wait for the ball. Sometimes, he will do a double catch in order to get a good grip. You may have to use a video camera to ascertain whether the trigger action is too fast or too slow. Of course, there are times when the dog will simply be sloppy and, consequently, bobble the catch.

Another thing that may contribute to a bobble at the box is your call timing. It could be that you are calling your dog too soon, thus encouraging an instant recall reaction before the dog has a grasp on the ball. If this is the case, go back to calling the dog once he has the ball and then work your timing to a suitable mark.

MISSING JUMPS

There are many reasons that contribute to dogs going around the jumps. In some cases, the jumps just aren't important to the dog. In this scenario, the problem is, once again, a breakdown in the behavior chain. The dog must be reeducated to understand that the hurdles are a necessary part of the game. If he goes around the jumps on the way down to the box, have the box loader cover the ball with his hand so that the dog doesn't get the ball. The dog needs to learn that if he goes around the jumps, he doesn't get the ball; but if he goes over the jumps, he does get the ball. Similarly, if the dog goes around the jumps on the runback, don't let him have the secondary motivator. He needs to learn that returning *over* the jumps is the route by which the secondary motivator is gained. Go back to your basic jumping lessons. Use your directed jumping hand signal to encourage your dog over the jumps. Then, backward chain the flyball course, as you did when you first put it all together.

Sometimes, an early exchange will cause a novice dog to go around the flyball jumps. This can happen in either direction (going on or coming off the course) and can affect one or more hurdles. I know I sound like a broken record, but the cure is to go back to the basics. Backward chain the course to help the dog regain his confidence and, when he's correctly running the course by himself, gradually reintroduce exchanges as discussed in Chapter 10.

In some cases, a dog will start going around jumps if the exchanges are taught and tightened too quickly. Always be sure that a dog is one hundred percent secure at each stage of an exchange before honing it further. And, when teaching your exchanges, run an experienced, non-threatening dog with the novice dog.

Often, a dog will start to go around the hurdles if you increase the jump height too fast and/or in too large an increment. Go back to a low jump height and work on your basic jumping skills. When the dog's reliability returns, raise your jump height once more, but this time do it slowly and in small (one-inch) increments.

Occasionally, you will come across a dog that, although he seems physically large enough to jump a higher hurdle, has difficulty in doing so. This dog will go around the jumps simply because the high hurdles are too hard for him to execute. In fairness to this dog, keep him in a team lineup with low jump heights. Flyball is not supposed to be a hardship for the dog.

ACTING NERVOUS WHEN MEASURED

The one element of flyball training that is most often neglected is the measuring of dogs. Being measured is part of the game and, therefore, something in which the dog should be schooled. I measure my dogs on a regular basis from the time they are quite young. After all, one can never be sure just how tall a dog will grow. It's better to get him used to being measured before it becomes a necessity. It's absolutely unfair to the dog to subject him to being measured if it's something that frightens him.

This is where your stand command lessons come in handy. Have your dog stand, practice stacking him properly, then teach him to stay (see Chapter 4) in a standing position. This shouldn't be difficult, if his basic stay has been well established. Once he can stand-stay, practice measuring him. Measure the dog from the floor to the withers (the junction of the shoulder blades). If moving his head up or down alters his height, you are not measuring him in the right place. Always be positive and be sure to praise him for correct behavior.

Aside from teaching your dog to be measured for a tournament (height dogs are measured before a tourney begins), it is important to be one hundred percent sure of his jump height for practice, because you need to practice at the correct jump height.

When you take your dog to be measured at a tournament (to establish his jump height), stand him up properly. Don't try to make him slouch so that he gets measured for a lower jump height; you will only set your dog and your team up for later disaster. Sooner or later, your dog will be measured correctly and your team will be required to jump higher on that day. It's not fair to your dog, or the other dogs on your team, to increase the jump height suddenly. Your dog could get hurt!

Your stand command lessons come in handy when teaching your dog to get accustomed to being measured. The dog should be measured from the floor to the withers. Photo by H. Kadish

13
Basic Rules of Racing

In North America, flyball is governed by NAFA. Its rules and policies were set out to benefit not only the sport of flyball, but also, and most importantly, to protect the welfare of the individual dogs racing under its provisions. Each team racing under NAFA's jurisdiction is assigned a NAFA number. Each dog is assigned a competition registration number (CRN), which is used to identify the dog for the points/titles system. As titles are achieved, NAFA provides certificates in recognition of the accomplishment.

THE FLYBALL COURSE

A flyball course is currently fifty-one feet in length. There is a ten-foot distance between each flyball jump, fifteen feet between the last jump and the box, and six feet between the start/finish line to the first hurdle. While the tournament host provides the jumps and flooring, each team is responsible for supplying its own flyball box and balls. A backup box is always good to have on hand. The current minimum jump height is eight inches and the maximum is sixteen inches. Your team's jump height is determined by the smallest dog in the racing lineup and is set to four inches below this dog's withers.

THE RACE

A race consists of either three or five heats (as decided by the tournament director) and a tournament generally follows either a round-robin or a double/single elimination format. Teams are divided into racing divisions, based on running times. Due to the large number of entries (and, therefore, divisions), most tournaments offer consolation rounds.

AWARDS

Ribbons for each division and consolation round are awarded according to the decisions made by the tournament director. For example, some tourneys may offer first-, second-, and third-place ribbons for all divisions and consolation rounds, while others may offer first place only to the consolation rounds, and some offer fourth-place awards. Seven ribbons are awarded per team, one for each of the six dogs/handlers and one for the box loader.

TOURNAMENT CLASSES

Tournaments are generally divided into regular and four-breed (or multi-breed) categories. In the regular classification, the team is not restricted in regard to how many of a given breed may compete in each lineup. In the multibreed classification, however, the rules state that each dog in the racing lineup shall be a different breed. Cross-bred dogs (mutts) are considered to be one breed. You can double up on a breed (e.g., have two Border Collies), as long as they never run in the same lineup.

TOURNAMENT TEAMS

As previously explained in Chapter 1, a *flyball team* is a group of people and dogs that play flyball together. The flyball team can consist of

Tournament						
Judge				Date		
Team	Northern Borders A			Division	One	
Captain	J. Parkin and D. McWhinnie			Phone		
Street Address						
City		State/Prov.		Zip/Postal Code		

Height Dog	Dog	Breed	Jump Height	Owner	Team # CRN	Points Per Dog
1	Ruffian	Jack Russell Terrier	10"	J. Parkin	059-940441	Accumulated
2	Shade	Border Collie	16"	V. Baldwin	059-930082	At
3	Casey	Border Collie	16"	M. Catherwood	059-930506	This
4	Kyle	Border Collie	16"	D. McWhinnie	059-940445	Particular
5	Davy	Border Collie	16"	D. McWhinnie	059-	Tourney
6	Aisling	Border Collie	16"	J. Parkin	059-940444	

Circle Which Dogs

Heat No.	of	vs						W L T	
Heat No. 1	of 3	vs Opposing	Dog 1 Are 3 Racing 6			Time Time	W L T	Win
Heat No. 2	of 3	vs	Dog 1 2 3 4 5 6	Time Of	W L T	
Heat No. 3	of 3	vs Team's	Dog 1 2 3 4 5 6	Time Each	W L T	Loss
Heat No. 1	of 3	vs	Dog 1 2 3 4 5 6	Time Heat	W L T	
Heat No. 2	of 3	vs Name	Dog 1 2 3 4 5 6	Time	W L T	Tie
Heat No. 3	of 3	vs	Dog 1 2 3 4 5 6	Time	W L T	
Heat No. 1	of 3	vs Goes	Dog 1 2 3 4 5 6	Time	W L T	
Heat No. 2	of 3	vs	Dog 1 2 3 4 5 6	Time	W L T	
Heat No. 3	of 3	vs Im	Dog 1 2 3 4 5 6	Time	W L T	
Heat No. 1	of 3	vs	Dog 1 2 3 4 5 6	Time	W L T	
Heat No. 2	of 3	vs This	Dog 1 2 3 4 5 6	Time	W L T	
Heat No. 3	of 3	vs	Dog 1 2 3 4 5 6	Time	W L T	
Heat No. 1	of 3	vs Column	Dog 1 2 3 4 5 6	Time	W L T	
Heat No. 2	of 3	vs	Dog 1 2 3 4 5 6	Time	W L T	
Heat No. 1	of 3	vs Stray Dogs	Dog (1)(2)(3)(4) 5 6	Time 18.01	(W) L T	
Heat No. 2	of 3	vs	Dog (1) 2 (3)(4)(5) 6	Time 18.05	W (L) T	
Heat No. 3	of 3	vs "	Dog (1) 2 3 (4)(5)(6)	Time 18.20	(W) L T	
Heat No. 1	of 3	vs Fastrack	Dog (1) 2 (3) 4 (5)(6)	Time 18.19	(W) L T	
Heat No. 2	of 3	vs "	Dog (1)(2) 3 (4) 5 (6)	Time 18.10	W (L) T	
Heat No. 3	of 3	vs "	Dog (1) 2 (3)(4) 5 (6)	Time 18.09	W (L) T	
Heat No. 1	of 3	vs k-9 Thunder	Dog (1)(2)(3)(4) 5 6	Time 18.03	W (L) T	
Heat No. 2	of 3	vs "	Dog (1) 2 (3) 4 (5)(6)	Time 18.14	(W) L T	
Heat No. 3	of 3	vs "	Dog (1)(2) 3 4 (5)(6)	Time 18.25	(W) L T	
Heat No. 1	of 3	vs Dog-On-It	Dog (1) 2 3 (4)(5) 6	Time 18.00	(W) L T	
Heat No. 2	of 3	vs "	Dog (1) 2 (3)(4)(5) 6	Time 18.16	(W) L T	
Heat No. 3	of 3	vs "	Dog (1)(2)(4)(5) 6	Time 18.22	(W) L T	
Heat No. 1	of 3	vs Northern Borders B	Dog (1) 2 (3)(4)(5) 6	Time 18.68	W (L) T	
Heat No. 2	of 3	vs "	Dog (1) 2 3 (4)(5)(6)	Time 18.59	W (L) T	
Heat No. 3	of 3	vs "	Dog (1)(2)(3)(4) 5 6	Time 18.15	(W) L T	
Heat No. 1	of 3	vs Fast Company	Dog (1)(2)(3) 5 6	Time 18.05	(W) L T	
Heat No. 2	of 3	vs "	Dog (1)(2)(3)(4) 5 (6)	Time 17.99	(W) L T	
Heat No. 3	of 3	vs "	Dog (1) 2 3 (4)(5)(6)	Time 18.09	(W) L T	
Heat No.	of	vs	Dog 1 2 3 4 5 6	Time	W L T	
Heat No.	of	vs	Dog 1 2 3 4 5 6	Time	W L T	

DIVISION: One   PLACE: _____   BEST TIME: 17.99

Sample tournament time sheet.

any number of people and dogs. In a tournament, however, you enter a *racing team*. Within the racing team, you have your *racing lineup*. You can enter more than one racing team to accommodate all of your flyball team members, but each racing team is restricted to six dogs. Four of the six dogs run in a racing lineup, and you are allowed to alternate dogs between heats.

A dog is only allowed to run on one racing team per tournament. Although he can move from one racing team to another between tournaments (e.g., he can run on Northern Borders A team at one tournament and on Northern Borders B team at the next tournament), he cannot run with more than one flyball team or club at one time. If you wish to change flyball teams, there is a four-month waiting period (from the last time that the dog raced in a sanctioned tournament) before being allowed to compete with a new group, unless you are forming a brand new team.

INFRACTIONS

As previously stated, in the racing lineup, you will run four dogs. The dog running onto the course must not cross the start/finish line before the dog coming off reaches this same mark. Nose to nose on the start/finish line is a perfect exchange. If, per chance, the dog going onto the course reaches the start/finish line ahead of the dog coming off, he will be flagged. In this case, the dog must rerun the flyball course at the end of the lineup. You are flagged either by the line judge or by the electronic passing lights (or both).

Because the rules state that the dog must run the course alone, the handler is not allowed to cross the start/finish line. Should you step across this line, you will be flagged and, therefore, required to rerun your dog. In a tournament in which the electronic passing lights are in use, you will be flagged if you wave your arms (or a motivational toy) across the start/finish line, because your arm (or toy) will pass through the sensors and trigger the passing lights. However, if one of your dogs knocks down a jump during a race, you are allowed to cross the start/finish line in order to reposition the hurdle. (If the electronic passing lights are in use, be sure to *go around*, *not through*, the start/finish line sensors!) Your dog will also be flagged and required to rerun the course if he drops the ball before crossing the start/finish line on his runback.

TITLES

Flyball titles are awarded on a point system. Each dog in the racing lineup is granted a certain number of points based on the cumulative team time. If the team completes a heat in less than twenty-four seconds, each dog in the lineup will be awarded twenty-five points. If the heat is completed in less than twenty-eight seconds, five points are awarded. One point is given for a heat completed in less than thirty-two seconds.

At the time of this writing, a dog must earn twenty points for a Flyball Dog title, one hundred points for a Flyball Dog Excellent title, and five hundred points for a Flyball Dog Champion title. Five thousand points are required for a Flyball Dog Master title, ten thousand points for a Flyball Dog Master Excellent title, and fifteen thousand points for a Flyball Dog Master Champion title. For dogs that earn twenty thousand points, NAFA awards the Onyx Plaque (named after its first recipient). A dog earning thirty thousand points is awarded the title of Flyball Dog Grand Champion.

INTERFERENCE

In the event that a dog from an opposing team crosses over into your racing lane during a heat, you win that particular heat by default. The judge will call interference. *Do not* release your dog onto the flyball course if there is a dog in your lane or at your box, regardless of whether or not the judge has already called interference. To do so could be dangerous for your dog.

Although you can and should use all sorts of motivators for your dog in training sessions, you must be sure not to distract opposing teams' dogs with these motivators during a tournament. For example, you are not allowed to throw a ball or Frisbee during a competition, as this could be considered interference.

As these are but the basic rules of racing, I strongly recommend that you obtain a NAFA rule book (or a book on rules that govern flyball in your country) for more detailed regulations.

Part 2

Honing Your Skills

14
Practice Makes Perfect

Many people think that once a behavior is learned, there is no need to continue training, but this is not so. Dancers, athletes, musicians, and singers all train continually in order to maintain peak performance levels. They do not only practice the dance, game play, musical score, or song currently being performed, but train daily in the basics of their chosen field. It is this continuous training that allows them to excel. And so it should be for our dogs. A dog that goes to obedience school for ten weeks does not stay trained for life if the lessons he has learned do not become a way of life. By the same token, a flyball dog does not remain fine-tuned in the game, unless the elements of the game are continually reinforced.

When the training of any behavior (in people and in their dogs) isn't reinforced and maintained, that behavior tends to extinguish or at least deteriorate in its level of performance. As I have witnessed, constant running of team lineups, without ever working on the elements of the game, can result in the decline of a dog's and/or the team's flyball performance.

It is too easy and too tempting to just stand back and run lineups once your dog is trained, especially if your dog is good! But many a good dog has reverted to a lesser performance level as the result of a lack of reinforcement and motivation in weekly training sessions. Invariably, the dog will lose motivation when the handler does. The dog will still play the game, because it is fun, but his *drive* will surely diminish. All too often, trainers fail to recognize *their* role in the dog's reduced mental drive. They blame the equipment, the weather, the flooring, etc., rather than take a close look at their training techniques. While things such as equipment, weather, and flooring can play a role in a dog's performance, consistent diminished drive is usually the result of a lack of motivation. And motivation is created by the handler.

A visitor to one of my teams' flyball practices was astonished at the physical effort the handlers put into the training. We run *with* the dogs, run away from the dogs, motivate the dogs, play tug-of-war with the dogs, wrestle with the dogs, and work with individual dogs. Sometimes, three people will work on motivating one dog. If a dog is having a problem, the whole team turns its attention to that dog. Flyball practice is exciting for our dogs! (My dogs run to the door of the practice hall and scratch on the door to be let *in!*) Before leaving, our guest shook his head and commented, "I'm so glad my dog is *beyond* this level of training. I don't have to run with him anymore. I can just let him go and toss a ball for him at the end." Well, you guessed it. This person does not run on one of the top teams in North America, nor is he ever likely to do so. At recent tournaments, this dog has shown a marked decline in performance and speed. The truth of the matter is this: *no dog is ever* beyond *the need for motivational training!*

Whenever working a behavior chain such as flyball, it is important to maintain each component in the chain. Behavior chains break down when there are weak links in the chain. For example, if you don't work on runbacks, your dog's runback speed will suffer; if you don't do box work, your dog's efficiency at the box will suffer.

Boredom is often the result of too much repetition (e.g., running lineups endlessly) and diminished performance is a definite symptom of boredom. Working *all* of the elements of the game creates variety for your dog and thus eliminates boredom. Trained dogs and flyball champions benefit positively from continued training of the elements of the game. It is in this way that you maintain and often improve performance.

15

Fine-Tuning Your
Box Work

T he box is probably the place where the most time is lost on the fly-ball course. *Ideally,* the dog should run off the box. The box shouldn't interrupt his execution of the course, but should propel him for the run-back. We generally refer to the desired turn off the box as a *swimmer's turn,* because the dog should push off the box with his back feet. However, his style at the box will determine whether or not a swimmer's turn is possible. Imagine, if you will, a skateboarder going back and forth on a U-shaped ramp. Visualize the turn he makes at the top end of the ramp. It's a tight U-turn. This is what you are trying to develop in the flyball dog.

Once your dog fully understands how to operate the flyball box and has chosen his side (right or left turning), you can begin to fine-tune his performance. Originally, I used a different exercise for each of my dogs depending on his or her particular needs. I then concluded that multiple exercises were of more benefit. Varied workouts conducted in a positive manner not only prevent boredom, but also make fine-tuning fun. Today, all of my dogs are trained with several fine-tuning lessons and are getting better results.

When you fine-tune your box work, you will not run the entire fly-ball course, but will concentrate exclusively on the use of the box. There should be no jumps on the course. If you are trying to change an estab-lished style, you need an average of two hundred repetitions of the new style before the new behavior becomes habitual. Remember, old habits

By fine-tuning your box work, the dog loses less time at the flyball box. Notice how this dog's feet are too low on the pedal to facilitate a swimmer's turn. This style causes stress to the shoulders and back. Photo by Zuma Press, Inc

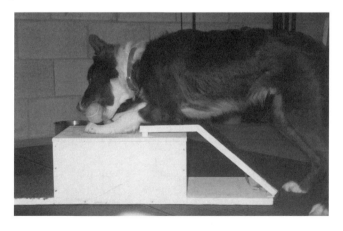

Murphy learned to play flyball on a box that required him to go up and over the top of the pedal to get the ball. This roachback style still haunts me today.

die hard! Murphy, for example, learned to play flyball on a box on which he had to go up and over the top to get the ball. This roachback style still haunts me today. Even though fine-tuning has greatly improved his efficiency and enormously bettered his style, I can still see that old roachback body posture creeping into his box work. Murphy and I continually practice at the box in order to maintain a decent turn.

Fine-tuning does help you to develop faster turns and better box style in a dog. However, don't expect instant results, because improvement (and especially change) requires time and work. Always cue your dog properly in timing and intonation when doing box work exercises.

THE PYLON

The pylon (an orange cone) is used to teach a dog how to make a U-turn. It is positioned in front of the flyball box at a distance of approximately two feet. Depending on the size and length of the dog, the distance may have to be slightly adjusted, because the dog needs to be able to fit between the box and the pylon.

The concept behind the pylon exercise is that the dog will run around the pylon, thereby making a U-turn. And, coincidently, he will

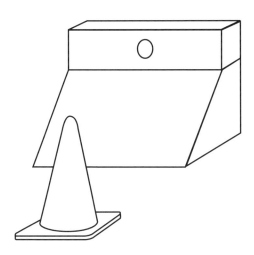

Use the pylon with the box to teach your dog to make a tight U-turn.

run on and off the flyball box, snatching the ball on his way. It is only by making this U-turn that the dog will be able to get his hind feet up onto the box for the push off.

Depending on which direction the dog turns, you will have to place the pylon ever so slightly to the left or to the right of the center of the box. If the dog turns right, position the pylon a tad to his right. If he turns left, position it a tad to his left. The reason for this is to allow the dog enough room to get his hind feet up on the box.

When teaching your dog the pylon exercise, forget about speed. With the dog on a six-foot leash, guide him to the box via the left side of the pylon (if he is a right-turning dog). When he triggers the pedal, guide him off to the right. Once he has a grasp of the exercise, guide him completely around the pylon. He will approach the box on the left side of the pylon and return past the right side of the pylon (from your point of view, looking at the box). Reverse this entire procedure for a left-turning dog.

This lesson teaches style, not speed. But, this style is necessary to achieve speed. As the dog's understanding and competence in negotiating the box (around the pylon) increases, so too will his speed. At this point, take him off leash and begin to do a nice runback. The next step is to slowly increase your send distance.

To teach the pylon exercise, guide the dog (in this instance, a right-turning dog) to the box via the left side of the pylon. Photo by H. Kadish

Once he triggers the pedal, guide the dog off to the right side of the box.
Photo by H. Kadish

Once the dog has a grasp of the exercise, guide him completely around the pylon. Reverse this entire procedure for a left-turning dog. Photo by H. Kadish

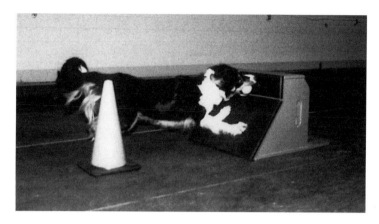

Once learned, the dog can perform the pylon exercise by himself.
Photos by H. Kadish

WINGS

Many dogs turn wide off the box. This interferes with their ability to gain momentum for the runback, because they need to scramble in order to get back in line with the jumps. A tight turn is the key to a smooth runback and wings encourage a compact turn.

Wings are boards (I use upended broad jumps) placed at the sides of the flyball box to form a chute. To begin, the wings should be positioned at a forty-five-degree angle to the box. When the dog is used to the presence of the wings, tighten the angle. I find that a twenty-degree to twenty-five-degree angle is sufficient for developing and maintaining a tight turn. Use wings whenever you practice.

Wings are boards placed at the sides of the flyball box to form a chute.

The size of a dog will determine just how tight he will be physically able to make the U-turn. Generally, a smaller dog is able to effect a tighter turn than a larger dog.

BOARDS

You can also use boards to help your dog develop and maintain a particular style. When strategically placed, boards encourage a change in box work.

For the dog that runs up too high on the box, hold a board at a thirty-five-degree angle over the top of the box. The mere presence of the board will encourage him to stay low. Make absolutely sure that the dog does not bang into the board. It is not meant to harm him in any way. As always, your send distance should be increased slowly.

If the dog is a pouncer, you can use a board to compel him to change his approach to the box. Place a board along the front of the box (left for a right-turning dog and right for a left-turning dog) so that it prevents the dog from pouncing on the box straight on. To avoid hitting the board, the dog has to position his feet in a manner that creates a better turn. This not only improves style and speed, but also protects his elbows and shoulders from the stress of slamming into the box.

For the dog who runs up too high on the box, hold a board at an angle over the top of the box.

A board strategically positioned across the front of the flyball box helps to alter the dog's style and use of the box.

Mudpuddles, a Rottweiler, used to come up lame as a result of pouncing on the flyball box. But training with boards altered her style and she no longer has a problem with sore shoulders.

THE BALL THROW AND PERIPHERAL VISION

The ball-throw exercise encourages a quicker turn off the box. It works best with dogs that are supermotivated for a second ball. The idea is that seeing the second ball will compel the dog to rotate quickly in order to obtain this reward.

To begin, position your dog in a sit-wait in front of the flyball box at a distance of approximately six feet. Then, position yourself to the side of the box to which your dog turns. Cue your dog to retrieve the ball and, once he is committed to this task, show him the second ball, holding it at the same level as the hole in the box. As soon as the dog triggers the box, place the second ball on the floor to the side of the box (at an angle of approximately forty-five degrees). This alerts him that there is a second ball in this new exercise. Next, place the second ball a little farther out in the direction of the dog's turn. Finally, throw the ball in the direction of the runback. (Remember, there are no jumps.)

As the dog becomes adept at this new lesson, alter the timing of your throw to when the dog is just about to trigger the box. He will see you throw the ball in his peripheral vision and this encourages a quicker rotation. Once again, gradually increase your send distance. (This exercise can also be conducted with a different secondary motivator [e.g., a toy or a Frisbee].)

THE RUNAWAY AND PERIPHERAL VISION

The runaway technique promotes a faster turn by capitalizing on the chase factor. Set your dog up in the same manner as for the ball throw and position yourself beside the flyball box (on the side to which your dog turns). As the dog triggers the box, run away as if you were running

Once the dog learns the ball-throw/peripheral vision exercise,
throw the second ball as the dog triggers the pedal.
Photo by H. Kadish

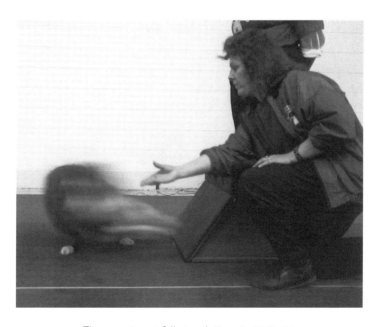

The exercise at full speed. Photo by H. Kadish

the entire course. Keep running until your dog catches you and play with him once he does. When he is proficient with this timing, encourage a faster turn by running away just as the dog is about to hit the box. The concept behind this exercise is that, in his peripheral vision, the dog will see you leave and will be compelled to spin off the box in order to chase you. Call the dog as you run away, with the same cue that you use in a race.

POPPING OFF

If your dog has a concrete understanding of the beat-the-pop game, you can use this exercise to promote a faster turn off the box. The dog will try to beat the pop by doing a superfast spin. Before you initiate a pop off the box, though, you need to be sure of the direction of your dog's turn. Again, your timing must coincide with the dog's action of triggering the box. As he does this, call him and pop him off the box to the side to which he turns. Do not pop straight back. Popping straight back could cause the dog to flip backward and fall, and possibly injure himself.

FIXING THE SLOW APPROACH

Often, a slow approach to the flyball box is caused by the dog being popped off the box. Many a young dog is popped off the box without having an understanding of the beat-the-pop game. In this instance, the pop off the box is interpreted by the dog as a correction for approaching the box. The result is a dog that is hesitant about retrieving the loaded ball, because he is never sure whether or not he will be corrected for doing so.

Border Collies with a strong eye often stick (pause) at the box. In this case, the dog slows to eye the ball as he approaches. This dog truly believes that he can *will* the ball to eject from the box! (I went through this with Murphy.) Anticipation of the callback and chase is another common cause for a slow approach to the flyball box.

Regardless of the cause, I have found that the cure for a slow approach is to cease concentrating on the turn. In fact, when I work with

Once your dog has a concrete understanding of the beat-the-pop game, use this exercise to promote a faster turn off the box. Photos by H. Kadish

a dog that has a slow approach, I direct all of my attention to the run-up and totally eliminate the runback. To do this, you simply run up to and past the box. Your dog will trigger the box as usual and you will continue to run. Once the exercise is established, have someone hold your dog and release him once you have a head start. The dog will approach with greater speed, because he will be chasing you and you will keep going. Be sure to cue the dog to get the ball, lest he become overexcited by the chase and forego the box altogether.

When the dog is converging on the box with confidence and without slowing, begin to piece the flyball course back together. However, you should not focus any attention on the runback—not until the dog is approaching the box with consistent speed. Only then should you start to press for quick turns and runbacks.

VIDEOTAPING

Videotaping is a super way to determine where a dog needs fine-tuning. Often, the action happens so quickly that it is difficult to ascertain what's going on at the box. However, watching the dog in slow motion provides incredible insight. If you have access to a video camera, take advantage of this wonderful tool. You will find it invaluable.

Photo by Jerry M. Thornton

16

Fine-Tuning Your Jumping

Many a dog's flyball performance is hindered by his jumping style, and many a jumping style is hindered by lack of attention to this area. For the purpose of flyball, you want your dog's jumping style to be as close to running as possible. There are several things that we, as trainers, can do to help our dogs develop and maintain a better, faster jumping ability. *You do not use the flyball box when fine-tuning your dog's jumping skills.*

RELEASE DISTANCE

Release distance, or lack thereof, is a major contributor to poor jumping. You need to determine the proper release distance for your dog to have a smooth and uninterrupted takeoff onto the flyball course. And, this release distance must be used consistently. If you are inconsistent with the distance from which you release your dog, he will never develop a comfortable stride and he will never be confident about his run onto the course. If you refer to Chapter 9, you will be reminded of how to determine and train for your dog's release distance. Always measure your release distance before practicing and never settle for anything less. It's not fair to your dog to expect him to adjust his stride constantly.

SINGLE STRIDING

The average medium-to-large-size dog generally starts to single stride the flyball course on his own as he gains speed and confidence. He will find double striding a nuisance and will naturally adjust his stride to a single step. However, there are some dogs that, although large enough to comfortably execute the ten-foot stride, have an inappropriate natural jumping style to accomplish this feat. It is these dogs that need to be taught to single stride.

Perhaps, I should clarify. Single striding is when the dog takes only one step between jumps. His landing from one leap is his takeoff for the next. Double striding is when the dog lands and then takes another step into the next hurdle.

Single striding is when the dog takes only one step between jumps.
His landing from one leap is his takeoff for the next.

Dogs that have a jumping style that arcs too high, land in a position that hinders their ability to take a single step into the next jump. The dog lands short of the center point between jumps and has a hard time making the leap over the next jump. Those that occasionally figure out how to single step usually have difficulty and often bash their knees on the jumps. The result is a tendency to go back to double striding the course.

So how do we teach this dog to single stride the course? We *change* his jumping style. We teach the dog to flatten out and not arc so high. He doesn't need to clear the jumps by six or seven inches. In fact, for

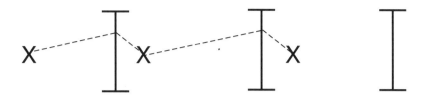

An incorrect jumping style for a single stride is when a dog lands short of the center point between the jumps and has a hard time making the leap over the next jump.

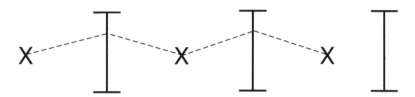

The correct jumping style for a single stride places the dog midway between the hurdles.

optimum performance, he should just skim over the jumps. Remember, even though he is jumping over hurdles, we want his jumping style to be as close to running as possible. You will notice that top-notch dogs that have been expertly trained and that run on consistently low jumps are not thinking in terms of jumping. They are *running*.

Now, the first thing I have to say on the retraining topic is this: You don't teach a dog to stride ten feet by putting the jumps seven feet apart! Many flyball clubs do this and will argue that their dogs have still learned to single stride. I beg to differ. The dogs that learn to single stride are those that would naturally single stride anyway. If you look closely at some of these groups of dogs, you will see double striders for which the seven-foot tactic has failed. Why? Because, once again, it is the dog's jumping style that is incorrect. By letting the dog stride seven feet, all you are doing is reinforcing a seven-foot stride. You aren't *teaching* the dog anything. The theory behind putting the jumps closer together is this: The dog will single stride the shorter distance and become accustomed to single striding. Therefore, as you slowly increase the distance to ten feet, the dog will continue to single stride, because he will have developed a habit of doing so. This is the method that I was told to use for my dog Shannon and I can assure you . . . it doesn't work! Why? Because the dog's jumping style does not facilitate a ten-foot stride.

To change a dog's jumping style, start by teaching him a simple broad jump. Photo by H. Kadish

So how do we change the dog's jumping style? It's not as difficult as you might imagine. You start by teaching the dog to do a simple broad jump. In order to accomplish the broad jump, the dog will flatten out. He will tend to do this naturally, because he can see that the jump has a distance to cover. Rev up your dog and throw a ball or a toy over the broad jump, if necessary, to motivate him to take the leap. Run with him (you're not doing a formal obedience broad jump) and make it fun. Once your dog understands and enjoys the broad jump, you can move on to the flyball jumps.

Make the row of four jumps a row of four broad jumps. Start with two jumps, then increase to three jumps, and finally all four. The dog needs to see that you want him to go over a broad jump, so that he knows to flatten out and reach for the landing point beyond the jump.

Broad Jumps   Hurdle

Always jump the dog toward the broad jumps, never from behind the flyball jumps.

Always jump him toward the broad jump, never from behind the fly-ball jumps, because the dog needs to be aware that there is a broad jump in place. From behind the flyball hurdle, he may not see the broad jump. If he takes the leap from behind the flyball hurdle, he may land *on* the broad jump and hurt or frighten himself. Remember, he has to *see* the jump distance in order to gauge his leap. Do this for some time, always motivating and praising your dog as you go.

When the dog is comfortably and consistently single striding the broad jumps, and you are confident that his jumping style has changed (become second nature) and will remain so without the aid of the broad jumps, take the broad jumps away. The dog should be single striding without conscious effort at this point.

Shannon played flyball for three years before learning to single stride. It was this method that taught her to do so and it only took two or three weeks of training. For the past four years, she has been single striding and increasing her speed. She has also come to enjoy the game even more, because it is less of an effort. Now, at the age of eleven years, Shannon is a better flyball dog than she was when she was young.

At eleven years of age, Shannon is a better
flyball dog now than she was when she was young!
Photo by D. McWhinnie

*If you don't have broad jumps, don't fret. When I trained Shannon,
I used garbage can lids!* Photo by H. Kadish

She started off at four years of age with a running time of 7.5–8 seconds. Now she runs 5.7–6.2 seconds. Not bad for a senior citizen!

If you don't have a set of broad jumps, there's no need to fret. Be imaginative. When I trained Shannon, I used garbage can lids and folded deck chairs to mark my broad jump distance.

Be aware that there are some dogs that, although they appear large enough to single stride, may never do so. A case in point is a dog on our flyball team. Skye is a small dog, only eighteen inches at the withers, and is very short backed and a little short on leg. It is her physical structure that prevents her from single striding the course consistently. In training her on the broad jumps, we discovered her physical limitations. On low jumps, Skye can single stride consistently, but when we increase the jump height she needs to double stride at least once on each run of the course. The single stride is difficult for her to execute, because in order to clear the higher hurdle, the highest point of the arc in her jump occurs at the end of her leap, which is directly over the hurdle. This causes her to land short of the center point between the jumps. If Skye were even one inch longer in back or taller on leg, she would be able to single stride comfortably.

So, when attempting to teach your dog to single stride, be aware of his physical capabilities and work within these confines. While you may never achieve consistent single striding at all jump heights, you can still improve overall performance. Skye went from a running time of 6 seconds on all jump heights, to a running time of 4.7–4.9 seconds on eight inches and 5.5 seconds on fourteen inches.

OVERJUMPING

Overjumping is most often caused when the jump height is raised too quickly or in increments that are too large. Other times, it is due to apprehension following a collision with a hurdle or a bash to the knees. And, of course, some dogs simply think they have to jump much higher than necessary. Regardless of the cause, we can usually fix an overjumping problem by lowering the jump height to a point at which jumping is not necessary, thereby encouraging the dog to run. Once the dog is thinking in terms of running, as opposed to jumping, you can begin to increase the jump height very slowly, staying at each new level for several weeks.

If the dog starts to overjump as the hurdles are raised, introduce the broad jump system, as just described. Often, a broad jump into the first hurdle only will do the trick. I used this method for Aisling. She used to clear the first hurdle by several inches and then flatten out, little by little, as she continued the course. However, by making the first jump a broad jump, she flattened out straightaway and ran the course with greater ease.

Tunnel jumping is another method of encouraging a dog to flatten out. Place a small hoop on each flyball jump or make each jump a hole-in-the-wall jump so that the dog is prevented from overjumping by the upper perimeter of the obstacle. Before applying this technique, however, the dog must learn to jump through a hoop or "hole in the wall." If you have enough handlers to help you with this exercise, you could use boards, held over each jump, or you can easily make a cardboard "hole in the wall" to fit your flyball jumps. The hole should be big enough for the dog to go through comfortably, but not so big as to allow him a six- or seven-inch clearance of the lower periphery.

STRIDING

Often, a dog will have difficulty executing the flyball course because his striding is off. For example, he may be a dog that can single stride, but his landing point makes this an arduous task and he occasionally knocks the jumps. What this dog needs is to change his striding! Sometimes, this is a simple case of helping the dog to change his point of takeoff. If that is the case, we can, once again, use a broad jump in

*Tunnel jumping through a hole-in-the-wall obstacle
encourages a dog to flatten out. He is prevented from
overjumping by the upper periphery of the obstacle.*

front of the first hurdle to assist the dog's performance. By placing a
broad jump in front of the first hurdle, we alter the dog's point of
launching so that his stride will fall in a more comfortable and, therefore, more efficient pattern. Determining the correct point for takeoff
may require a few adjustments to the positioning of the broad jump, but
it's well worth the effort if it helps the dog. Once you have discovered
the correct placement for your broad jump, be sure to measure the distance from the first hurdle, so that you can place this training tool in
position for every practice run until this new and improved striding is
one hundred percent habitual. If you are using this technique, you will
have to remove the broad jump as soon as the dog is on course, so that
it is not in the way of his teammates or himself as he runs off the course.

RUNNING RESTRAINTS

Running restraints are valuable exercises because they build mental
and physical drive in your dog's jumping attitude. In fact, my team
starts every practice with this exercise. Have someone restrain your

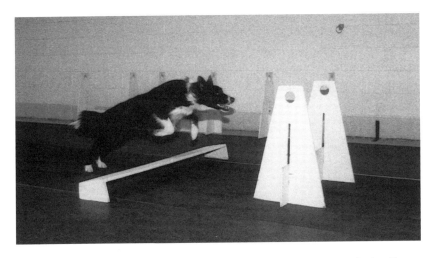

A broad jump in front of the first hurdle alters the dog's point of takeoff.
Therefore, his stride will fall in a more comfortable and efficient pattern.
Photo by H. Kadish

dog while you run away with a secondary motivator. When you are about half to three-quarters of the way along the row of jumps, call your dog and keep running until he catches you. Be sure to make it worth his while when he does catch you. Running restraints not only encourage the dog to run fast and in a determined fashion, but also reinforce handler focus.

INCREASING THE JUMP HEIGHT

Always increase the jump height in very small increments and remain at each new level for several weeks. Rushing not only promotes over-jumping, but also increases the dog's chance for injury, loss of mental drive, and loss of speed. As you adjust the jump height, be sure to evaluate the dog's striding to make certain it is correct, comfortable, and efficient. Do lots of running restraints to build speed and confidence. Only when the dog is one hundred percent consistent on one jump height should you raise it. If the dog is having trouble with the new height, go back to the lower level. It could be that he is too young to cope with the increased height or it is too difficult for him at this stage of his training.

The greatest challenge to a dog's ability to run and jump at the same time, is the urgency the trainer places on him to perform. When you are increasing jump height, you work on jumping first, then speed, then jumping, then speed. Never ask for speed when the dog first goes to a new jump height.

POWER JUMPING

Power jumping is best done in a park where you have lots of running space. I learned the true value of power jumping when my team was in its infancy. We didn't have a flyball box for a few months and instead of taking a break from our flyball training, we decided to work on our dogs' jumping skills. Our goal was to build power and stamina. So, off to the Georgetown Fairgrounds we went and we worked on power jumping our dogs.

Power jumping follows the same format as a running restraint with two exceptions. First, you call the dog when you reach the end of the jumps, and second, you throw a ball or a Frisbee as far as you can (farther out from the jumps) once the dog reaches you. Not only is the dog super revved up for chasing you, but he runs an additional thirty to fifty feet past you to retrieve the ball or Frisbee. Once he has the secondary motivator, run away again so that he chases you and catches you for a game and praise. The dogs love this game and it really boosts their morale.

The idea behind having the dog run past you at top speed is to teach him to run off the course at full tilt. And, as always, with repetition, this behavior becomes habitual. It was this power-jumping that helped Kep gain control of his awkward puppy self and develop a strong, fast running and jumping ability. In fact, all of the dogs on our team benefitted enormously from these power-jumping sessions.

Building stamina for jumping can be achieved by increasing the number of hurdles from four to eight. Do this gradually, adding one hurdle at a time and be sure that the ground is level. Follow the same format as before—the dog chases you, then chases the ball or Frisbee, then catches you. The incredible distance that the dog can run in a park or fairgrounds is what makes the difference between a simple running restraint and power jumping.

HESITANT APPROACH TO THE COURSE

A dog's approach to the flyball course directly affects his jumping ability on the course. If your dog has a hesitant approach to the course, it could be that his striding is off and he's not comfortable with the point of takeoff. As with a slow approach to the box, videotaping and/or assistants can help you to determine if this is the cause. If so, you will have to make adjustments either in the dog's release distance or point of launching.

Another reason for a slow approach could be intimidation. If your dog feels at all intimidated by the dog coming off the course, he will not summon the courage to run past this dog. You will have to go back to really loose exchanges and build his confidence. Sometimes, if exchanges have been taught and/or tightened too quickly, the dog will be unsure of running into another dog. Run with your dog and motivate him onto the course, so that he is focused on the task at hand and not on the other dog.

Photo by H. Kadish

17

Putting Fine-Tuned Elements Together

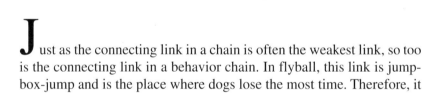

J ust as the connecting link in a chain is often the weakest link, so too is the connecting link in a behavior chain. In flyball, this link is jump-box-jump and is the place where dogs lose the most time. Therefore, it is this connecting behavior that we have to be certain not to neglect.

Many dogs lose momentum once they hit the box. What I generally observe is dogs that don't quite kick into gear until they are halfway home. The connecting link is weak. These dogs need to learn to go from "zero to sixty" in less than two seconds! (The superfast, top-notch flyball dogs perform this link in 1.6 seconds!) They need to accelerate mentally and physically immediately on triggering the box. Part of that action is dependent on good box work and the other component is attitude.

In many cases, a dog doesn't kick into gear until he focuses on his secondary motivator, which he often doesn't see until he is halfway home. Therefore, we need to teach him to expect it sooner. By concentrating solely on the connecting behavior, we can promote instant acceleration, thereby strengthening the link and, subsequently, overall flyball performance.

To strengthen this link, you have to work on jump-box-jump. Send your dog over one hurdle to retrieve the ball from the flyball box. As he turns off the box, immediately show him his secondary motivator. Because the secondary motivator is only twenty feet from the box rather than fifty-one feet, it provides a more instant reward and the incentive to

By concentrating on the connecting link, the dog learns to expect his secondary motivator sooner and therefore shifts into overdrive straightaway.

shift into overdrive straightaway. With time, this instantaneous shift into overdrive will become habitual and, when you are certain that it has, add a second hurdle, and then a third, and finally a fourth. Backward chain the course as you did when the dog was first learning. Do not add hurdles until the connecting link is consistently strong and fast. The dog shouldn't slow down at the box. His speed, whatever it may be, should remain constant.

Once you have strengthened the connecting link and have accrued the full four-jump runback, you can adjust the exercise slightly to maintain the behavior. When you release your dog to run the course, run halfway down the course yourself (alongside the jumps) and, as he turns off the box, call him and run away while showing him his secondary motivator. In this way, he will see the object right away and will follow it off the course.

You can also use the chase factor to encourage maintenance of the connecting link. In this exercise, position yourself beside the jump closest to the flyball box and have an assistant release your dog onto the course. Call your dog. As he takes the final jump in his approach to the flyball box, run away and call him off the box. If it is unlikely that you will be able to outrun your dog, have your assistant (who is at the start/finish line) call him as well and show him his secondary motivator.

To determine your dog's performance of the connecting link, you need to use a stopwatch. Activate the stopwatch as soon as the dog's nose reaches the upright of the hurdle approaching the box. Stop the watch as soon as his nose reaches the same upright on the way back. Your goal is to have your dog perform the connecting link in less than two seconds.

Photo by Zuma Press, Inc.

18

Better Exchanges

Accuracy in your release timing for exchanges is probably the most difficult task for the handler. A moment too soon and you'll be early. A moment too late and you could lose the race. It's a lot of pressure. However, if you have a concrete formula to calculate your release, your chances of rendering a decent exchange will be greatly increased.

The basic release timing as described in Chapter 10 is suitable for most dogs of comparable speeds. However, when running dogs of varying speeds or superior velocity, you have to make adjustments in your timing.

THE STOPWATCH

One of the best ways to determine the ideal release timing for a perfect exchange is to use a stopwatch. Measure and mark (on the floor) each foot of the flyball course, as well as your release distances. Use brightly colored duct tape to make these marks, so that you have a clearly defined visual reference from which to work. Now time the dog running onto the course from his point of release to the start/finish line. Then time the dog coming off the course from the point in his run at which his distance from the start/finish line equals the release distance of the dog running onto the course. (Run each dog separately. You are not doing exchanges right now, but simply calculating the correct timing.) This will give you an idea whether the dog going onto the course needs to be released earlier or later. Continue to time the dog coming off the flyball course (from different points in his runback) until you determine the exact point at which both dogs are at an *equal* time distance from the start/finish line. This is the point at which you should release the dog going onto the course. This system is, of course, most suited to dogs with consistent running times—not necessarily fast, but consistent.

VIDEOTAPING

If at all possible, videotape your exchanges during practice in order to determine their accuracy correctly. The faster the dogs and the closer you sit to the start/finish line, the harder it is for the human eye to determine the exchange.

With the use of a video camera, you not only benefit from watching your exchange in slow motion, but you are also provided with an excellent tool for honing your skills as a line judge—something at which all members of your team should become proficient. At a tournament, it is invaluable to have a fellow team member watch your exchanges and coach you from the line. However, at a tournament in which electronic passing lights are not in use, this coach is often prohibited from calling the exchanges aloud, lest it interfere with the line judge's perceptions.

MULTIPLE HUMAN MOTIVATORS

Sometimes, exchanges are impaired by a dog's uncertainty about running onto the course while another dog runs off. Often, this uncertainty is the result of teaching and tightening exchanges too quickly. Revert to loose exchanges and build the dog's confidence. Don't tighten the exchange until the dog is completely unaffected by the presence of the other dog and even then, only tighten it in small degrees.

Use multiple human motivators to focus and encourage the dog as he approaches the flyball course. Position one assistant by the first jump and a second assistant approximately halfway down the course (each on either side of the hurdles in order to be more visible to the dog). Have an experienced dog run the course ahead of the dog in training. As the first dog is running back, the first assistant should call to your dog in order to distract his attention from the other dog. Then, as your dog begins to run onto the course, the second assistant should begin to call him as well. Have both assistants run the course with the dog, giving him lots of encouragement. Your goal is to build his courage and confidence in approaching the flyball course. It is only in this way that his run onto the course will be consistent enough to effect a good exchange.

Use multiple human motivators to focus and encourage the dog as he approaches the flyball course.

Photo by Zuma Press, Inc.

19
Getting a Good Start

Handler timing and canine body posture are both important factors in procuring a good start. In competition, a good start is the beginning (hopefully) of a good race. Without a good start, you will be behind and trying to catch up from the outset.

Just as the human competitive runner requires a proper racing stance before takeoff, so too does your flyball dog. Make sure that his weight is centered and his footing secure. While there is no doubt that straddling the dog provides an excellent preparatory stance for racing, this handler positioning is sometimes too intimidating for certain dogs. The greatest myth in flyball is that a fast dog must be straddled. This is not so. You can start your dog just as effectively by holding his collar.

STRADDLE START

The purpose of straddling the dog is to provide him with a good, solid starting gate from which he can gain acceleration for his run onto the flyball course. To become this human launching pad, begin by standing your dog between your legs, then place your foot behind the dog's corresponding hind foot so that his leg and foot are braced against your lower leg. Let your other leg remain alongside the dog's body. Next, hold the dog by his chest and shoulders so that he can lean forward into

The straddle start position. Photo by H. Kadish

your hands. Don't claw him with your fingers, just cup your hands so that he is leaning into your palms. Release the dog by simply letting go of him at the appropriate time. He will propel himself by pushing off your leg with his hind foot.

When I tell Murphy to line up, he automatically positions himself between my legs. As soon as I take hold of his chest and shoulders, he braces himself for the race. You can teach your dog this behavior quite simply. Every time you take him into line say, "Line up!" and he will associate the cue with the behavior. Teach him to pull forward into your hands by having an assistant bounce a ball for him. Cue him with "Ready!" and when he's revved up, release him to chase the ball. He will quickly learn what *ready* means.

COLLAR RELEASE

For the submissive dog that is intimidated by the staddle release, use a collar hold. Stand alongside your dog and hold on to him by the handle

The collar release starting position. Photo by H. Kadish

on his flyball collar. Teach him to brace himself for the race in the same manner as described for the straddle. If possible, bend over to coach your dog with racing cue words, but if this is still too dominant for your dog, crouch down beside him. Whatever you do, don't use his collar to throw him over the start line! You'll throw him off balance and it looks awful to the spectators. If he needs to be physically pushed or thrown over the start line, there is something seriously wrong with your training program.

SMALL-DOG RELEASE

Depending on how small your dog is, you may or may not be able to execute a standard collar release for his run onto the course. However, you can modify this release technique ever so slightly by simply kneeling down.

You can also modify the human launching pad for your small dog. Kneel down and let your dog push off your knees or lap.

The small-dog release. Photo by H. Kadish

DON'T LEAN

Regardless of the starting method used, make sure that your dog is not leaning to one side, because this will interfere with his takeoff. If he is leaning to one side, he will stagger a step or two to regain his balance. Often, leaning is the result of lining up in single file in preparation for a race. The dog leans to one side in an effort to see past his teammates and this leaning eventually becomes habitual. If this is the case with your dog, don't line him up directly behind another dog. Instead, stand him to one side so that he can see the race and move into place when it's his turn.

To break the leaning habit, alter (often only temporarily) your beginning stance. Remove whatever part of yourself the dog is leaning away from or against. For example, if you are holding his collar and he's leaning away from you, let go. He'll soon learn not to depend on you to keep his balance. If you are doing a straddle start and the dog is leaning to one side, remove the hand holding the bulk of the weight. If he's leaning sideways into your leg, move it. Don't provide him with anything on

*Don't lean! If the dog is leaning to one side,
he will stagger a step or two to regain his balance and
this will interfere with his takeoff.* Photo by H. Kadish

which to lean. Encourage him to stand well balanced on his own four feet! The only direction in which he should lean or pull is forward.

THE JUDGE'S START

As with exchanges, the stopwatch is the best way to calculate a perfect start. In North America, NAFA rules dictate that the head judge adhere to a consistent starting tempo of approximately one-second intervals. However, since there is always room for human error, I advise timing the judge's starting cadence at the beginning of a tournament. Before you attend, know your start dog's time from point of release to the start/finish line. Then calculate the proper release timing if need be. In training, practice your starts based on a one-second interval in the starting rhythm.

THE START LIGHTS

If you are attending a tournament at which the electronic starting lights are in use, you can reliably time your release based on one-second intervals. The judge will make eye contact with you to see if you are ready and then she will activate the start lights. Keep your eyes on the yellow lights, because these are your get ready and get set lights. The dog should reach the start/finish line *as* the green light (the go light) illuminates. Depending on the speed of the dog you are running, you will have to release your dog with either the get ready or get set lights—or somewhere in between the two. For example, I release Murphy a heartbeat *after* the get set light; I release Aisling *with* the get set light.

20
Evaluating Individual Dogs

By evaluating an individual dog's performance and assessing his strengths and weaknesses, you can determine the areas of his presentation on which to concentrate and discover areas in which the dog may be limited. It is this personal training that enables the dog to reach his full potential.

In practice, take time to appraise each dog carefully as he runs the course. Check his striding. Is it smooth and powerful? Check his jumping style. Is he arcing too high? Check his exchanges. Are they confident? These are the type of questions you must ponder in your role as K-9 coach.

PHYSICAL ABILITY

It is very important to be aware of your dog's physical limitations. Remember Skye, the Border Collie I spoke about in Chapter 16? It is her physical structure that prevents her from consistent single striding. This knowledge protects Skye from being pushed to perform a task that she is incapable of performing and allows her trainer to direct attention to other areas of her performance. For example, Skye does dynamite box work.

To assume that your dog can perform at a certain level based on others of his breed is unfair. Not all dogs of the same breed have the same talent for flyball. I have five Border Collies. The quickest runs in just over four seconds and the slowest runs in just under five seconds. Ruffian, the Jack Russell Terrier, has a best running time, to date, of 4.6 seconds. This is not typical of his breed, but he's a very talented individual. Many small dogs cannot achieve running times under five seconds simply by virtue of their size. You have to be realistic about what a dog can accomplish and encourage each dog to work to his full potential. Success should be measured by accomplishments made based on an individual dog's ability. I believe it is very wrong to measure success in seconds.

PHYSICAL CONDITION AND STAMINA

Flyball practice once a week does not a canine athlete make! In fact, it's almost cruel to demand peak performance of him if this is the only real exercise he gets. Imagine how you would feel if you were to go to the gym tomorrow and work out after having led a sedentary life for some time. You would be exhausted and sore! Your muscles would say, "Hello! What did we do to deserve this abuse?" Well folks, it's no different for our dogs. They may not be able to tell us that their muscles are aching, but if your dogs are used to spending seven days a week snoozing on the sofa, their dreams interrupted only for meals and a short walk, these poor dogs are destined to be sore. If you want to play competitive flyball with your dog and you want him to be the best that he can be, you need to treat him like an athlete. He needs daily conditioning exercises and good nutrition. And he absolutely must not be under- or overweight!

Flyball practice once a week is not how to attain or maintain fitness in your dog. Your dog must engage in some sort of fitness program on a daily basis and there are many activities in which you can participate. Hiking, jogging, biking, swimming, and playing ball or Frisbee are all obvious choices. Retrieving on a sandy beach, or in the snow, or on a hill (not too steep) are also excellent conditioning exercises. Alternate dog sports (such as lure coursing, terrier racing, sledding, and herding) can also contribute greatly to the fitness level and stamina of your flyball dog. It is only through being fit and healthy that your dog can, in all fairness, be expected to excel.

Whatever your fitness program, embark on it gradually, just as you would if beginning a workout for yourself. Try to include activities that enhance both strength and stamina. Although strengthening exercises,

Your dog must engage in some sort of fitness program on a daily basis.

Swimming and retrieving are good conditioning exercises.

Dog sports such as herding and agility also provide excellent conditioning. Bottom photo by H. Kadish

which develop the fast-twitch muscle fibers, are of great importance to a flyball dog, be careful not to neglect exercises that develop slow-twitch muscle fibers and, thus, enhance your dog's level of endurance. Strength is required for speed, while running, jumping, and stamina are required for a long day of racing.

My dogs engage in a fitness program that includes biking (running alongside the bicycle) a distance of approximately two kilometers each day, daily Frisbee or ball retrieval on sandy ground, and swimming at least three times per week.

MENTAL DRIVE

Although mental drive is largely an inherent characteristic in our dogs, we can, through training, enhance this personality trait and overall flyball performance. Assess your dog's attitude. Is he submissive? Does he stress easily? Or is he a real go-getter? Knowing these things will help you to work more effectively with your dog by enabling you to tailor your training regime to suit his personal needs. For example, with a more submissive dog you may not want to employ a straddle start technique. Building confidence is the key to enhancing mental drive; positive training techniques are the key to building confidence.

It is only by being fit and healthy that your dog can,
in all fairness, be expected to excel.

PRIOR TRAINING

Your dog's prior training and methods of training play a significant role in his flyball education and performance. Awareness of your dog's prior training and how it positively or negatively affects his flyball instruction is of great importance. This knowledge provides invaluable insight when solving behavioral or training problems. Dog X is a case in point of flyball training gone wrong. He required a great deal of retraining in order to correct problems caused by his prior education. Dog X was trained to believe that speed was all important and he was not instructed properly in the elements of the game. With speed foremost in his mind, Dog X began to go around the jumps to retrieve the ball more quickly. In an effort to correct this, the box loader would yell at Dog X and chase him away from the box. The result? Dog X became apprehensive about approaching the box and refused to leave his trainer. The problem was then compounded by the trainer's frustration. Dog X was stressed "to the max." He didn't understand what he was doing wrong and all efforts made to correct the problem simply made it worse.

What was needed in this situation was a complete break from formal flyball and a return to better, more positive basics. Dog X needed to relearn the elements of the game, with a total disassociation from his prior training. He needed to regain confidence in his ability to make the right decisions. Only through reeducation and understanding was he able to do so.

Without knowledge of his prior training and the effect it had on him, Dog X would not have been able to succeed. So you see, awareness of a dog's prior training (whether it be flyball or obedience) is paramount in assessing his performance and helping him to succeed.

FLEXIBILITY

When I speak of flexibility, I am referring to the dog's ability to run in any position in the lineup, without prejudice toward specific breeds and/or other dogs on his team. A flexible flyball dog is invaluable to a team's success, because he is reliable wherever he is needed in the team lineup. You don't need to worry about him. This dog is more valuable than your fastest dog, if the latter can only run in one position or has breed prejudices. Therefore, your flyball training should include teaching the dogs to be flexible and sociable. This can be done through group hikes, obedience training, and changing the order of the team lineups periodically. Young pups should attend puppy kindergarten classes in order to learn to be dog social.

Here, the author helps her dog focus, prior to being released onto the course.

21

You As a
Handler/Trainer

A dog is usually only as good as the human on the end of his leash. All too often, we blame the dog for things lacking in his performance, when, in fact, he is merely reflecting his trainer's effort and ability—or lack thereof. Just as a cut rose will wither and die without nurturing, so too will untapped talent. You as the handler/trainer are responsible for nurturing the dog's raw talent and bringing it to fruition.

ANIMATION

Animation is a key factor in creating and maintaining a positive learning environment for your dog. Your attitude will greatly affect his ability to learn and become successful. Always conduct your training sessions with a positive attitude. If you are feeling stressed, irritable, short-tempered, or impatient, train your dog when you're feeling better.

You need to be animated so that learning is fun for your dog. Being with you has to be more fun than chasing other dogs. If you are dull and boring to your dog, so are the lessons you are teaching.

CONSISTENCY AND TIMING

Whether teaching new lessons or reviewing established behaviors, it is necessary to be consistent. Always use the same commands and body language. *Don't* change the rules. Lack of consistency creates confusion, confusion creates stress, and stress interferes with a dog's ability to learn. Consistency brings faster, better, and more reliable results.

A facet of consistency is timing. Do you always call your dog at the same time for his runbacks? Are you good at timing your exchanges? Do you always reveal your secondary motivator at the same point in your dog's run? These are some of the questions to ask yourself. As a handler, you will be an asset to your team if you possess good timing. But developing consistent, good timing takes practice. By being aware of your handling skills, you will be better able to acquire the dexterity needed to become a top-notch handler with great timing.

FLEXIBILITY

As a team player, it is important to be flexible. For example, you should know how to start, how to do exchanges, how to watch the line (coach your team's exchanges), and how to time the dogs. You should be able and willing to lend support to fellow handlers and dogs, and, if need be, be able to run a dog other than your own. In addition to all of this, you should be able to act as box loader or team captain, in the event of your captain's absence. You need to be able to function in any and every capacity of the team.

PHYSICAL CONDITION

Although you are not actually running the entire flyball course yourself, it is a grave misconception to believe that the sport requires no physical effort on your part. (Just being animated can exhaust a lot of energy.) If you are physically incapable of running with the dog and encouraging the chase, you will not be able to develop the same fast chase as the handler who *can* run. Your fitness level definitely plays a role in training and maintaining peak performance in your dog. When my back is sore, I can hardly walk, let alone run with my dogs, and there is a marked decline in their performance. Because of my lack of animation and physical effort, my dogs don't receive the motivation they need to reach peak performance. Since the game is fun and they love to play, they still run the course with decent times, but not to the best of their ability. At times such as these, a friend usually steps in and either runs my dogs for me or motivates them on the course.

REACTION UNDER PRESSURE

Your reaction under pressure is another factor that affects not only your dog's performance, but also your team's performance. If you get really uptight at a tournament, you communicate this stress to your dog and he also becomes stressed. This stress interferes with his ability to perform at peak levels.

Your handling skills are also affected by your reaction under pressure. Many a race has been lost due to an early or late exchange that results when a handler cracks under pressure.

Although it's much easier said than done, learn to focus your attention on the task at hand and not on the environment. In this way, you can keep your cool when nervous.

WATCH OTHER HANDLERS

One of the best ways to improve your handling skills is to watch other handlers. When you see a fabulous flyball dog, observe his handler. Evaluate this person to discover what she is doing to contribute to the performance of the dog, because a good dog invariably has a good handler. Watch not only what she does when running the dog, but also what takes place when the dog comes back. Discover what makes this person successful and try to emulate her. There is much to be learned through watching others.

BE INNOVATIVE

To become a good handler, you must be innovative. If traditional training methods aren't working, try something new. The techniques I share with you in this book are the results of innovation—innovation born from experience, trial, and error.

Awareness is the key to everything you do as a handler and will help you to become innovative. For example, my team had a dog in training that was terribly distracted by the presence of a flyball box in the opposite lane. We tried conventional training methods to eliminate this behavior (we ran him on a Flexi-lead, spotted him in case he went off course, ran alongside him, etc.) and he was fine, as long as we did all of these things. However, when given the chance to run the course independently, he crossed over to the other box. Finally, we asked ourselves, what variable never changes. The answer was obvious—the box loader. In competition, there is always a box loader standing on the opposing team's box. Now we knew how to fix this dog's problem—make the box loader a slightly whacky character who is *very* possessive of her flyball box! The idea was to make the dog believe that the box loader in the opposing lane was someone to be avoided! From this point on, until the dog became reliable, we always had a box and box loader in the opposing lane during practice. Now the dog is one hundred percent reliable.

CONSERVE YOUR DOG'S ENERGY

During your dog's flyball training, try to discourage hyperactive, pre-race hysteria. All that bouncing and barking wastes energy. The poor dog will be exhausted before the actual race starts. Now I know that this is easier said than done, but it *can* be accomplished. Teach your dog to lie down and wait. Or teach him to simply be with you. If you observe the top racing teams, you will notice that the dogs do not waste energy by bouncing and barking. For the most part, these dogs just mill around their handlers and/or lie down. As evidenced by their spectacular performance, they are no less excited than the canine that is hysterically leaping around on the end of his leash, but they are more focused and in tune with the task at hand.

PROVIDE WARM-UP AND COOLDOWN TIMES

Always be sure to provide your dog with ample warm-up and cool-down times. Don't take him from his crate directly to the racing lanes. Walk him around for a few minutes and, if there are stairs available, walk him up and down the stairs a few times. This simple activity will limber up his muscles without tiring him for the upcoming race. If you can manage to teach the dog to stretch on command, this will also provide a good warm-up exercise.

Following the race, please avoid immediately crating your dog. He needs cooldown time in order to prevent muscles from cramping and to allow his cardiovascular system to return gradually to a resting state. Walk him around for a few minutes and offer him a small drink. Wait for his panting to slow down and, if it is summer, cool him down with a dousing of cool *(never cold)* water. Most clubs hosting summer tournaments provide a water hose and/or wading pool for this purpose. If you do water down your dog, please remember to be considerate of others requiring this shared facility and be considerate of those preparing to race. Never take your dripping wet dog into the racing area, because the footing in the racing lanes must always be dry for safety. Always be sure that your own dog's feet are dry before racing.

DON'T BE COMPETITIVE TO A FAULT

Do you run dogs on painkillers so that they may continue to race? Do you keep your brood bitches on Ovaban so they won't miss a tournament by going into heat? Do you use treatments such as acupuncture and laser therapy as tools to ease the pain from an injury temporarily, rather than keep the dog out of competition for a few months and let the injury heal? (While we don't see many injuries resulting from fly-ball, dogs *do* get injured in life and these injuries must be allowed to heal fully before resuming flyball practice and/or competition.) Do you run dogs of medium and large breeds at five and six months of age on fourteen-, fifteen-, or sixteen-inch jumps? Have you ever gotten rid of a dog because he couldn't play flyball? Have you ever bought or cho-sen a dog (or breed of dog) specifically for the purpose of flyball and no other reason?

If you can answer yes to any one of these questions, you have become competitive to a fault. The dog has become nothing more than a tool of the trade. And this, my friends, is shameful!

A dog is a living, feeling being. He deserves better than an owner who views him merely as a flyball commodity. He deserves better than to *become* a flyball commodity.

Most people don't start off in flyball (or any dog sport) as overly competitive individuals. But, somehow, competition has a way of taking control of one's priorities. The result is that the once happy family dog becomes nothing but a source of glorification for the owner. Suddenly, the dog's worth is judged by his flyball performance. If he's not good enough, a new dog comes along and takes his place. This is *wrong!*

Hopefully you're reading this and saying to yourself, "I can't believe that people can be that competitive." Well, believe it. It hap-pens in all aspects of canine competition. People choose the sport over the dog. Be appalled. Don't become competitive to a fault. Make sure that you and your dog have a life and appreciate each other outside the sport of flyball.

22

Organizing a Team

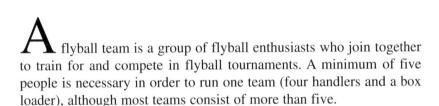

Aflyball team is a group of flyball enthusiasts who join together to train for and compete in flyball tournaments. A minimum of five people is necessary in order to run one team (four handlers and a box loader), although most teams consist of more than five.

If interested in forming a flyball team, it is necessary to recruit members. There are a few ways in which to pursue this goal. One way is to attend a flyball class and approach fellow students about forming a team, once you all have learned the gist of the game. Or, if your dog is already trained, you could *watch* a flyball class and invite potential members from that source. Not all schools, clubs, and teams that offer classes have available space on their teams for new members. Often, an individual will attend a flyball course only to find nowhere to turn once the course is completed. Of course, if you are an experienced flyball enthusiast you could conduct your own flyball lessons and acquire teammates from your students. Still another avenue is to use the flyball newsletter in your area. You could place an ad stating that you would like to form a team in your area.

The success of the team depends largely on the people involved, even more so than the dogs involved. If the people on the team clash, it won't matter how good the dogs are, because the team will not be in harmony. When selecting potential team members, be sure to look past the dog to the *person* who will be joining your group.

Most flyball teams practice once a week as a group and these practices generally consist of training and fine-tuning the elements of the game that are either difficult or impossible to train alone. However, it is important to remember that many elements of the game (e.g., directed jumping, chase and handler focus, basic retrieving, etc.), as well as keeping your dog fit, are things that can and should be done at home.

If the rental of a practice area is not possible right away, there's no need to postpone active team participation. Simply practice in a park or fairground until a hall becomes available. When my team first came together, this is exactly what we did. We found a park central to all members and met once a week for group practice.

Naturally, team spirit is a must and the success of the team depends on all participants having a common goal. The team must be in sync in order to succeed. For this reason, no good is derived from forcing an individual (through guilt trips or other types of manipulation) to remain with the team just because her dog might be an asset. Each dog and handler is a team in itself. If the human partner is not allied one hundred percent with your flyball team's goals, that dog and handler unit will not function to the benefit of the team. The unhappy handler will pull down team morale, flyball will *not* be a positive experience, and the team will *not* flourish.

When people join my team, they are told up front, "If this is not the right team for you, you're free to leave. No hard feelings." We don't expect that the Northern Borders team will be right for everyone and it's not worth losing friends over flyball. Remember, it's a game. It's supposed to be fun!

No matter how much the departure of one member will damage your team (we lost our height dog at one point), you *will* survive. You may be slower for a while, but you *will* survive. There are other good dogs! Never allow one dog or one person to manipulate the team. Ultimately, it will make everyone miserable.

Give people the freedom to leave your team if they're not happy. As hard as it may be at the time, try to understand that perhaps it just wasn't meant to be. Things have a way of working out for the best. It's an evolution, of sorts. Enjoy the sport, run with people who share your objectives, be successful, and, above all, enjoy your dogs.

Now, occasionally, it will happen that your dog, your only dog, will not take to flyball, but *you* want to be involved. Don't fret. There are other ways in which you can become a valuable member of a team. For example, you could be a full-time box loader or you could run a dog belonging to someone else on the team who has multiple dogs. You could be a coach, a video camera operator, a statistics person, or a fund raiser. There are all sorts of capacities in which you can become involved with flyball. I became involved in the sport through my dogs, but my co-captain originally became involved as a box loader (and now she has four flyball dogs).

CHOOSING A TEAM NAME

As new teams continue to enter the league, new names are continually being sought and it's not always an easy task to pick one, let me tell you. My co-captain and I tossed about several (and many silly) ideas before settling upon Northern Borders.

People choose different names for different reasons. There are those named after obedience schools or clubs, others that suggest speed, and some that indicate the geographical area from which the team origi-nates. So what is the meaning and motivation behind the Northern Borders' name?

1. Our team consists predominantly of Border Collies.
2. Our non-Border Collie breeds (at the time of the team's founding) were northern breeds and cross-northern breeds.
3. We hail from north of the Canadian border.

Thus, Northern Borders!

When choosing a name, it is advisable to secure a copy of the offi-cial flyball newsletter in your area so that you will know which names are already in use.

CHOOSING A LOGO AND TEAM COLOR

The best way for me to help you in choosing a logo and team color is, once again, to tell you how it all came to pass with my team. At the time of my team's inception, no one else was wearing purple (at least, not that we knew of), so we chose purple as our team color. Our logo, a Border Collie leaping over an igloo, ties into our team name. Here's a rundown of how it came about:

The Northern Borders' team logo.

1. The Border Collie represents our many dogs of this breed.
2. He is jumping, because flyball entails running and jumping.
3. The igloo represents the Great White North (as Canada is often referred).
4. The Border Collie is wearing a scarf blowing in the wind, which denotes speed.
5. The maple leaf, which appears after the team name written on the scarf, represents Canada.

DEMOS

Demos are an excellent means of raising funds for your flyball team. Five hundred dollars per day is not an unreasonable amount to earn, providing your demo is good, involves more than just flyball, and is presented two to three times daily.

I consider a minimum group of eleven people necessary to put on a good demo. For the flyball demo alone, you require this number (eight dogs and handlers [for two teams of four], two box loaders, and an emcee).

Your demo equipment doesn't need to be fancy, but it should be clean and pleasing to the eye.

Always remember that a demo is entertainment—showbiz! It is not a training session for dogs that are not well schooled or that are unfamiliar with the equipment and/or events to be performed. A dog that is going to go off course and chase other dogs or not come when he is called is not yet sufficiently trained to be part of a demo. However, a green dog can gain experience at a demo. If necessary, the handler can run alongside him and coach him.

When putting on a demo, make sure that all participants are well groomed (people *and* dogs) and that all are outfitted in a uniform manner (i.e., team outfits). Your equipment doesn't need to be fancy, but it should be clean and pleasing to the eye. Music is a great asset. It can make the dogs look faster, add suspense to a difficult trick, have a comedic effect for a silly trick or goofy-looking dog, and add overall excitement to your show. Choose fast-paced, upbeat tunes that enhance the events you perform.

When planning flyball for a demo, you do not necessarily group your teams as you would for a competition. It's not exciting for your audience to see one team wipe the other off the face of the earth. Instead, group your teams equally, so that the race will be close and more exciting for your audience. Exchanges are not important and it doesn't matter which team wins. Remember, it's a show. Keep the dogs as evenly matched as possible.

What I generally do when running the flyball portion of the Northern Borders' demo is name the teams the red team and the blue team (one set of jumps has red stanchions and the other has blue). Then I divide the audience into cheering sections for each team and encourage them to cheer by telling them that the louder they cheer, the faster the dogs will run. We run four heats, alternating wins, and then run a fifth heat as a tiebreaker. The emcee does a play-by-play call of the race, thereby adding excitement to the performance.

Your demo should run thirty-five to forty minutes and should keep moving throughout. A basic demo could include the following:

- a small agility course
- Frisbee catching
- tricks
- flyball
- high jumping

A good demo is a great crowd pleaser and an asset to any local fair or animal event. Write a proposal that describes your demo and send it to the appropriate events coordinator.

SPONSORSHIP

Running a flyball team can be a costly endeavor. You need equipment, team shirts and jackets, a place to practice, and, most importantly, money for tournament entry fees. Entry fees can run from seventy to one hundred dollars per racing team for a sanctioned event and approximately twenty-five to forty dollars per racing team for a nonsanctioned event.

Sponsorship, if you can get it, is the way to go. The degree of sponsorship available varies from one corporation to the next. For example, some pet food companies will offer a token sponsorship in the way of dog food for your team dogs. Others will provide team shirts and jackets, while still others will provide full sponsorship for your team. Pet food companies are not the only sources for sponsorship. Any business that can benefit from having its name displayed in public is a potential sponsor for your team.

The biggest faux pas made by most teams in their search for sponsorship is the "we want" approach. An attitude of superiority (a you-need-us approach) will shut the door to negotiations quicker than anything else. Always remember that when searching for sponsorship, *you* need *them!*

Potential sponsors need to know what's in this deal for them. They need to know *why* they should sponsor a flyball team, *what* they will gain from sponsoring a flyball team, *why* they should choose *your* team, *what* you can offer them in terms of exposure for their product or company. Lastly, they need to know the degree of sponsorship you are seeking. Never ask for a dollar figure first. Sell the idea, pique their interest, then discuss finances. Send a neat, professionally written proposal, addressed to the correct person, to the potential sponsor.

Once you have secured sponsorship, you are obliged to represent your sponsor in a professional manner at all times. This entails everything from a tidy appearance to being sportsmanlike at tournaments. Sponsorship is not a matter of "take the money and run." It is a marriage, of sorts, and both partners must work to keep the relationship healthy. A good sponsor is to be greatly appreciated and not taken for granted.

ENTERING A TOURNAMENT

The best way to find out about tournaments is to subscribe to the official flyball newsletter in your area. In North America, this publication is called *The Finish Line* and you can obtain information on how to subscribe through NAFA (see Other Sources of Information at the end of this book). The newsletter contains a list of upcoming tournaments as well as the current flyball team seedings for your country. It will also have tournament results, news articles, and ads pertaining to flyball.

In North America, all dogs wishing to compete in a sanctioned flyball event *must* have a CRN. This number must be obtained *before* attending a tournament. For information regarding entering tournaments for your group, contact NAFA or the governing flyball association in your country.

HOUSE LEAGUE

The Brampton Obedience School in Brampton, Ontario, runs a unique off-season activity—a flyball house league in which individual teams compete every Sunday. Approximately twenty-four teams enter the league and a round-robin format is followed, with six teams racing on a given day.

In this house league, teams are allowed four core dogs and four alternates. This gives participants a chance to try out new dogs in a tournamentlike atmosphere. However, if a dog is run on a Flexi-lead or on a lower than regulation jump height, the team forfeits that particular heat. For example, when Ruffian first completed his training and was assigned a position on the team, we ran him in the house league. In this way, he gained experience before going to a sanctioned tournament. Initially, because he had never run amid the kind of excitement that real competition generates, we chose to forfeit a few races so that we could run alongside him and keep him focused.

That's the great thing about the house league. It generates the same excitement for the dogs as a sanctioned event. The difference, of course, is that you cannot forfeit races in order to train your dog in a sanctioned tourney. There is no way to simulate the excitement of competition. The flyball house league, however, provides real competition while still allowing teams the opportunity to train to a small degree.

House league teams are also called on to do their share of the judging. In this way, participants become well acquainted with official flyball rules, get a taste of what it is like to be a judge (something that aids in one's appreciation of these officials at a sanctioned tournament), and experience camaraderie. The teams entered in the league judge each other, which encourages fairness. After all, the team you judge this time may be judging you on the next Sunday that you run. The schedule is designed so that each Sunday, one of the teams not racing on that day will be assigned to judge.

In addition to the training and competition benefits, the flyball house league is a great place to get to know other teams, to make friends, to network, and to help each other with flyball-related concerns. Teams helping teams. What a great idea!

At the end of the season, the play-offs are held. Teams are divided into divisions and seeded accordingly. Ribbons are awarded for first, second, and third place in each division, and a winner's plaque is displayed at the Brampton Obedience School. The flyball house league season generally runs from November until the end of April—a time when there is not an abundance of sanctioned tournaments to attend. For information on how to run a flyball house league, contact the Brampton Obedience School (see Other Sources of Information at the end of this book).

HOSTING A TOURNAMENT

Hosting a flyball tournament is a tremendous undertaking. You need to select a tournament committee and chairperson; secure a location and date for the event; provide all the necessary equipment, flooring, and awards; decide on the format you wish to follow and whether or not you wish to conduct a limited or unlimited tournament; select judges and apply for a sanction (both of which need to be approved by the governing flyball association); advertise the event; decide on the cost of entry fees; and send out tournament entry forms.

And that's just the beginning! You also have to be responsible for setting up and tearing down the racing lanes, cleaning the tournament site, operating a food concession (if not in a location where food concessions are already available), and paying the judges. Then, when the tournament is all over, it's still not over! The final job is to submit complete records of the tournament to the governing body so that team seedings can be correctly maintained and points toward titles awarded.

As you can see, running a tournament is not a stroll in the park. However, most governing bodies (such at NAFA) are willing to help you organize an event in any way possible. For official rules pertaining to the organization of a flyball tournament, contact the governing flyball association in your country.

23

The Team As a Unit

S uccessful flyball racing requires successful teamwork. Just as the instruments in an orchestra must play in harmony, so too must the members of a flyball team. The team must operate smoothly and as a single unit. This is not an individual dog sport.

THE ELECTRONIC LIGHTING SYSTEM

The electronic lighting system used in flyball was created and designed by John Peters of Clarkston, Michigan. The inspiration was born of a need to reduce and eliminate false starts in the sport of flyball. John was acutely aware of the arduous task imposed on the line judges in determining a dog's presence on or before a particular point—in this case, the start line. In a time frame of hundredths of a second, the line judges must employ both visual and aural senses (watch the line and listen for the whistle) to determine a false start or early exchange.

The timing of the light sequence was adopted from NAFA judge Dave Samuels, whose starting cadence follows a one-second chronology. The rising and falling of his arm signals a get ready, get set, and go. This one-second time delay was set to a succession of lights of different

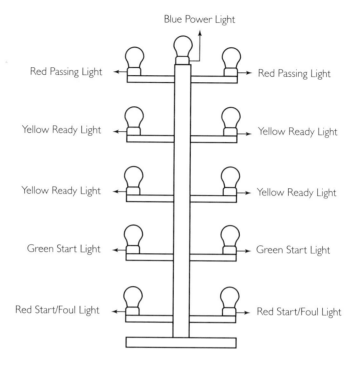

Blue Power Light

Red Passing Light

Red Passing Light

Yellow Ready Light

Yellow Ready Light

Yellow Ready Light

Yellow Ready Light

Green Start Light

Green Start Light

Red Start/Foul Light

Red Start/Foul Light

colors. Currently dubbed *the starting tree*, the system assumed this label because of its likeness to an illuminated Christmas tree.

The centermost light at the top of the tree is blue and remains on at all times, indicating that electric power is being supplied and the system is operational. Beneath the blue light there are two columns of lights, one for each racing lane.

The first, outermost light down from the top is red and its purpose is to indicate false exchanges. It illuminates in the column corresponding to the lane in which the infraction occurred. The second light is yellow and, when illuminated, is considered to be the get ready signal. The third light is also yellow and it functions as the get set indicator. It is activated one second after the first yellow light. The fourth light in the sequence illuminates one second later and is green; it signals "go!"

The lights at the base of the starting tree are red. These lights will illuminate if the first dog on the team reaches the starting line before the green light is visual or activated. This indicates a false start and a restart is set up by the head judge.

The accuracy of the system is ensured by infrared electronic motion sensors positioned at the starting line. Because of the accuracy of this technology, human error is eliminated. (This alleviates the burden placed on the line judges.) The sensors also display the digital timing indicators used to monitor a team's elapsed time. The sensors indicate the passing motion of the last dog to cross the finish line and, at that point, the clocks are stopped.

With the elimination of human mediation, nose-to-nose exchanges become a reality and false calls are eliminated. We who compete in the sport of flyball owe a debt of gratitude to John Peters for his dedication and expertise in developing the electronic lighting and timing system.

LINEUPS

There are a few common strategies that you can employ to determine a lineup:

1. Run your small dog first, thereby letting the other team take the lead and acquire a feeling of security and confidence. (The idea behind this strategy is that they will relax their exchanges because they have the lead.) Then, run your three fastest dogs and snatch the lead from them.
2. Run your slowest dog first, for the same reasons as strategy #1.
3. Run your fastest dog first in order to establish a lead and push your opponents into playing catch-up. The idea behind this strategy is that they will push too hard and will be flagged for an early exchange.

On my team, we simply try to concentrate on our own dogs and what we're doing, rather than play mind games with opposing teams. Time spent worrying about other teams could be better spent focusing attention on one's own team. We choose lineups according to which dogs run best in which positions. Some dogs are better start dogs than others, while others are revved up by the dogs running ahead of them. Some dogs turn into total space cadets if they have to wait in line to run. These dogs are better off in start positions. Other good start dogs are those that run faster when presented with a clear run onto the course (no dog coming off the course). And some dogs make good anchor dogs, because of the clear run off the course (no dog coming onto the course). In a close race, a dog that gets revved up by the cheering of the crowd also serves as a good anchor dog. Sometimes, the size of the dog can play a role as well. We usually run Kep in the anchor position, because he's big and doesn't leave much room for a dog to pass him to get onto the course. As you can see, there are many factors to consider when choosing your lineups. Sometimes the dog with the least-consistent speed is your best anchor dog, because this is a difficult dog behind which to get a good exchange.

All of our dogs can race in any position and this is an important factor for which to train, because sometimes things change and the dogs have to be adaptable. For example, we were competing at a tournament in Detroit when one of our dogs was injured. Our original lineup was Ben, Murphy, Tikka, and Kep. Suddenly, we had to change the lineup when we put our backup dog in. The lineup became Bess, Ben, Murphy, and Kep. Bess is not usually a start dog and Ben usually runs better in first spot. However, with a handler who had never run a Border Collie before (let alone Bess), and who had no idea of our team's exchange timing, it was easier to put him and Bess in the first spot and coach him on the starts (a member of another team was kind enough to step in to help us out). The planned lineup changed, and the dogs and handlers had to be adaptable. If we had dogs that could only run in one position, we would have had to forfeit the remainder of the tournament.

While it is true that some dogs prefer certain positions, it is important for them to learn all positions. (Remember, be flexible!) Sometimes, this can be beneficial to the dog's performance, because when presented with his favorite spot, the game becomes more exciting and he performs better.

Initially, many novice dogs will have a problem with certain positions in the lineup and, unfortunately, handlers often accept this problem as a reason to have a dog that can only race in one spot. I very often hear comments like, "Jack has to run first," or "Jack has to run last," or "Jack doesn't like Bill." These kinds of things really complicate a team. Imagine trying to arrange a team lineup based on who likes who and around dogs that can only run first or last!

Although it is easier not to have to train a dog to run in a position he doesn't like, you must do so. You might find that once this barrier is overcome, you have a dog that will run better in a new position. For example, a dog that doesn't like to pass going onto the course, may turn out to be a good anchor dog. But you'll never know if you don't train the dog to pass going onto the course!

Some people feel that a green dog must always run last, probably because they are afraid that he will follow another dog back over the jumps. I disagree. I have found that it all depends on the individual dog. If the dog is properly trained and has a good strong comeback and stays focused on the handler, it shouldn't matter in which position he runs. Sometimes a green dog is better off running the starts. Aisling is a good example. Aisling was very distracted by dogs coming off the course and had a lot of trouble learning to pass going onto the course. For this reason, when she first started competing, she ran as our start dog. Because she had a good comeback and was focused on me, it was more beneficial to the team to run her first and get a good, tight exchange behind her, than to run her last with a poor or possibly nonexistent exchange.

Another point to ponder when deciding on lineups is this: Your start dog should be a dog with good stamina, especially if you are racing in the championship division. Early starts could mean that your start dog will have to run twice the number of runs as your other dogs. If he doesn't have good stamina, you will surely lose speed. Generally, we try to have two start dogs of equal speed. This way, we can alternate in the event of multiple false starts.

The timing of releases for the handlers is another factor in determining lineups. Some people are just more talented than others in getting good exchanges. Therefore, if your dogs are all equal as far as being start dogs are concerned, it is sometimes beneficial to put the person with poor exchange timing in the first spot. With the use of the starting lights, starting is easier to learn than exchanges. For this reason, it is also a good spot to put a green handler. Why is the start easier? Because the lights are consistent, which means that the timing is consistent. When running behind another dog, there is a margin of inconsistency. The dog may not run at *exactly* the same speed on every run; the dog may bobble at the box or may not have a good grip on the ball (which would cause him to run slower, because he's concentrating on not dropping the ball). The handler doing exchanges has to learn to read the dog coming off the course and be able to make slight adjustments in the timing of the release in the event that a dog is running slightly slower or faster.

When deciding your lineups, try to remember that every position is an important one. Your anchor dog doesn't have to be your fastest dog and your start dog shouldn't be slated as your slowest or weakest dog. (This is a very old way of thinking.) These kinds of labels only serve to create discouragement on the one hand and immense ego on the other. *Every dog and handler on the team is important.* In order to function effectively as a team, everyone must feel that she is making a valuable contribution. There is no glory spot! No one dog wins the race. The race is won by the cumulative efforts of all dogs and handlers on the team.

ORGANIZATION

Arguments ensue when there is no defined *leader* to make final decisions. Too many chiefs and not enough Indians will set the team up for trouble. My co-captain and I make most of the decisions, but not without input from the team. We review lineups again and again to come up with what we feel is best for the team as a whole, and we don't attach any stigma to A or B teams. We are very fortunate to have members who are not hung up on the A team versus the B team, and we afford the same amount of consideration to each team lineup. All handlers and their dogs are important members of the team.

Organization is necessary in order to run practices efficiently. Have a plan to help keep you on track. Decide ahead of time the lineups you are going to run at the next tournament and practice those lineups. (Believe it or not, I have spoken to people who didn't know in which lineup their dog was running until the morning of a tourney!)

Organization also extends to keeping team records and entering tournaments. Consult with team members as soon as a new tournament is posted in order to ascertain who is available and secure your entries. In a limited tournament, it is important to enter early if you wish to have the chance to run more than one racing team.

When at a tournament, organization helps keep your team informed. Arrive early enough to let your dogs settle in and to have your height dogs measured. Make sure you have your official racing sheets completed and you are aware of any special rules pertaining to that tournament. Keep your flowcharts handy so that all members of the team can remain aware of the races and be ready to go when it's the team's turn. When it is the team's turn to race, organization helps you to utilize your warm-up time efficiently. Plan ahead and assign individuals to set the jump heights, collect the ball buckets, and help with warm-ups.

Otherwise, you'll be awfully surprised at how quickly your allotted warm-up time will go by.

COMMUNICATION

Communication is of tremendous importance when running a flyball team and team input should always be encouraged. Every member of your team has something to offer and the sharing of ideas strengthens the unit. Never arbitrarily shoot down another's opinion. If you strongly disagree, ask yourself why and then express your reasons in a civil manner. In this way, no one is offended and brainstorming is possible. The lines of communication should always be open, even when it comes to an individual wanting to leave the team.

WATCH YOUR TEMPER

Temper serves no useful purpose. There's no point in chastising teammates for early and/or late exchanges in a race. No one deliberately tries to be early or late. It's an accident and we are all guilty of this error. If you want to race with really tight exchanges you can't be afraid of being early, but you will surely be apprehensive if there is a probability of a teammate losing his temper. By the same token, if you feel that you're going to be yelled at for a late exchange, you might push too hard and be flagged for an early one! So, you see, temper will interfere with the team's success.

TEAM SPIRIT

Team spirit is always important when running a flyball team, and a positive team attitude takes the group a lot farther along the road to success than a negative attitude. Members need to feel appreciated and confident in the team's abilities (and so do the captains—don't take them for granted!) Try to focus on attainable goals and don't judge yourselves based on the achievements of others. For example, set a goal to beat your own record time rather than fret over not being able to break the world record (unless, of course, breaking the world record is within your grasp). By setting attainable goals, the team will be successful and team spirit will flourish. Remember, don't measure success in seconds only. Success is the achievements made by your team at its current level of expertise.

AVOID BOREDOM

Boredom is a great contributor to failing team spirit. It's hard to be enthusiastic when you are bored. However, you can avoid boredom for both handler and dog by eliminating too much repetition from your practices. Don't just work lineups. Work the elements of the game in a positive and highly motivational manner. Set realistic goals for your dogs and yourselves, so that you can feel successful and happy with your progress.

Social interaction between handlers and dogs also helps to alleviate boredom. Allow the dogs some free playtime and social time following practice. They can mingle while you're cleaning up, for example. Of course, they should be dogs that get along! On my team, we have several intact males (stud dogs) and bitches, as well as the spayed and neutered crew, and we don't have a problem with canine interaction and socialization. Even those that are "top dogs" at home, do not assume any status on neutral territory. This social acceptance of one another allows them to enjoy free time. Free time for the handlers can be a cup of coffee and a chat session at a local restaurant or donut shop. After all, socialization is important for us too!

PLAY FAIR

Whether at a flyball tournament or at practice, try to play fair. There is no satisfaction to be gained from cheating. While some may call it strategy, there is often a fine line between the two. For example, when the electronic start lights first came into use, a small dog could be taught to duck when crossing the line and therefore not be caught by the sensors for an early start. Armed with this discovery, individuals were able to train for early starts . . . and a few did. It was called *strategy*. However, in the eyes of the majority of flyball competitors, it was called *cheating*. Where would you draw the line? In my opinion, whenever you conspire to gain an unfair advantage over your opponents, you are cheating. Taking the time to teach a dog to scoot under the sensors deliberately, for the express purpose of getting a jump start on the race, is definitely conspiring to gain an unfair advantage. Fortunately, keen eyes saw these early starts, confirmed them on video, alerted the designer of the system (who had himself noticed an infraction), and the sensors were immediately adjusted to prevent this "strategy" from continuing.

Play fair. It's more fun to win a ribbon you deserve.

THE BOX LOADER

Often, the most forgotten member of the team is the box loader. In fact, at one time, ribbons were only issued for the dogs and handlers on the team. The box loader was unrecognized. Today, however, the role of the box loader is fully recognized and most teams realize how important this individual is to the performance of the dogs.

Your box loader is responsible not only for loading the tennis balls, but also for giving verbal motivation to the dogs. At the 1992 Pedigree Christmas Flyball Classic, held at the Credit Valley Dog Show, Aisling made her debut on our A team. She ran faster than I had imagined possible. So much so, that the person running behind us had to completely reevaluate her exchange timing. She kept saying, "What's happening to Aisling? She keeps getting faster!" (Her fastest time, taken from video, was 4.31 seconds over fourteen-inch hurdles.) The *box loader* was what was happening to Aisling. He called her onto the course with such enthusiasm that I could hardly hang on to her, and when she got down to the box, he told her, "Go, go, go!" My dog was revved up to the max! All of our dogs just fed off the fervor of the box loader. He made a significant difference to our team, because he was motivated, enthusiastic, and excited about the performance of the team.

Your box loader has the power to affect a dog's performance immensely. For example, a growling, menacing tone of voice (yes, some do come across this way) might be interpreted as very threatening to the dog and may serve to intimidate rather than motivate. Therefore, it is very important to be aware of tone of voice. In fact, with a submissive dog, it is sometimes better to be silent as he approaches the box. In practice, you can experiment to determine what is best for each dog.

So you see, the job of the box loader entails much more than you might imagine. He or she must be aware of tone of voice; know each dog by name; know which hole to load for which dog (if you are using a multiholed box); know which size of ball to load for which dog; know which verbal cues go with which dog; know if there's a rerun and, if so, which dog is rerunning; know if a dog is getting reckless and tell him "Easy!" if need be; and recognize any problems a dog might be having and inform the handler.

OUT-OF-TOWN TOURNEYS

When traveling to an out-of-town tournament, I would advise driving to the tourney location a day ahead of time. In this way, you can ensure that you and your dogs will be well rested before the tournament begins. Many competitions begin at eight or nine o'clock in the morning, so imagine how early you would have to set out in order to arrive on time. When I refer to an out-of-town tourney, I am alluding to a driving distance of more than three hours (e.g., traveling from Toronto to Michigan). Being awake and refreshed after a good night's sleep is of tremendous importance to both dogs and handlers, but it is most critical for the dogs. After all, they are the ones required to expend the most energy.

Aside from the obvious benefit of rest, traveling a day ahead of time is also a safety precaution. What if your car breaks down? What if there's a holdup at the border? What if you get lost? Any or all of these situations could prevent you from making it to a tournament, if you are driving to it the same day. However, driving a day early (or even the night before, after you leave work) will allow you the opportunity to contact a team member for help or to make last-minute alterations in the team's planned racing lineups.

TOURNAMENT CHECKLIST

Now that you have learned to play flyball and are ready to compete, I wish you *good luck* and leave you with this checklist of things to pack when going to a tournament:

- dogs
- crates
- water bowls
- leashes
- flyball collars
- motivational toys
- baggies (remember to stoop and scoop)
- Show Foot or Tacky Paw (in case the racing surface is slippery)
- towels (in case of inclement weather, dry the dogs' feet before racing)
- dog food and bowls (for out-of-town tourneys)
- lawn chair
- team NAFA number and CRNs (or whatever is applicable under the governing association)
- small fan and extension cord or batteries (for summer tourneys)
- tarps and beach umbrellas (for outdoor summer tourneys)
- vaccine certificates (for crossing the Canadian border)
- video camera
- stopwatch
- money (don't forget to change currency, if necessary)
- team shirts and jackets
- sponsorship banner (if applicable)
- map of area to which you will be traveling
- first aid kit
- flyball boxes
- balls and ball buckets

Note: Make hotel arrangements well in advance and be sure to ascertain whether or not dogs are welcome.

About the Author

Jacqueline Parkin was born in England and moved to Canada at five years of age. Educated at Loretto Abbey in Toronto, Jacqueline, a professional dancer, choreographer, and teacher, was headed for a long career in showbiz when she was sidelined by a cute canine and, as her mother puts it, "went to the dogs—literally." Jacqueline is a freelance writer on the subject of—what else?—animals. She has been involved in canine education for more than fourteen years and has titled nine flyball dogs of her own. She has worked for veterinarians, is the founder and director of Canadian Animal Actors and Casting, and trains animals for movies, commercials, and still photography.

This is Jacqueline's first, full-length book. She is currently working on her second.

Jacqueline lives in the Georgian Bay area of historic Huronia, Ontario.

The author with her flyball dogs.

Glossary of Terms

ANCHOR DOG	the fourth dog in the racing lineup
BAIT	the action of drawing a dog into a certain position by having him follow a food lure
BFA	the acronym for the British Flyball Association
BOBBLE	when the dog drops the ball at the box or has a bad catch at the box
BOX LOADER	the person who loads the tennis ball into the flyball box
BRITISH FLYBALL ASSOCIATION	the governing body for flyball in England
BUMPER	a canvas-covered item used to train retrievers
COLLAR CORRECTION	a firm pop on the leash that directs the dog's attention away from an undesired source
EXCHANGE	refers to the point at which dogs pass one another at the start/finish line
FLAGGED	when the judge observes an infraction and raises a red flag to indicate an error

FLEXI-LEAD	a retractable leash
FLYBALL	a sport in which dogs race over a series of four hurdles to retrieve a tennis ball
FLYBALL BOX	a box with a pedal on the front that releases a tennis ball when activated by the dog
FLYBALLER	a flyball enthusiast
GREEN DOG	an inexperienced, yet fully trained dog
HAMMER	the mechanism in the flyball box that thrusts the ball forward and out of the box
HANDLER	the person who runs the dog in competition and/or practice
HEIGHT DOG	the dog in the racing lineup that sets the jump height for the team
JUNIOR HANDLER	a handler under the age of eighteen years
LEADING LEG	the leg that leads the dog's stride
LINE JUDGE	the person who sits and watches the start/finish line for early exchanges, and who records which dogs ran in which heats
LONG LINE	a lightweight long cord (such as drapery cord) that is approximately twenty feet in length
NAFA	the abbreviation for the North American Flyball Association
NORTH AMERICAN FLYBALL ASSOCIATION	the governing body for flyball in North America
PATTERN	the act of teaching a dog a behavior pattern
POP	a quick, unexpected jerk on the leash
POSITIVE REINFORCEMENT	a style of training through praise and reward, as opposed to force
RACE	a series of three or five heats

RECALL   when the dog goes to the handler when called

RELEASE LINE   the visual mark used to indicate the distance at which the dog is released to run the flyball course

RERUN   when the dog has to run again, at the end of the lineup, because of an infraction

RUNBACK   when the dog races to the handler from the flyball box

SIDE   the direction of the dog's turn off the box

SINGLE STRIDING   when the dog takes only one step between flyball jumps

STACKING   the act of standing the dog up straight and square

STICK   when the dog pauses at the box

STRIDE/STRIDING   the pattern of the dog's running/jumping style

SWIMMER'S TURN   a turn off the box in which the dog pushes off the box with his back feet in the same manner that a swimmer pushes off the wall of a pool

TEAM   a group of people and dogs who play together

TOURNAMENT   an event at which various flyball teams compete for ribbons and points toward titles

TOURNEY   another word for tournament

UPRIGHTS   the stanchions that support the flyball jumps

WITHERS   the ridge of the shoulder blades, which forms the highest point of the back

Other Sources of Information

North American Flyball Association
P.O. Box 8
Mount Hope, Ontario
L0R 1W0 Canada

For information on flyball rules, equipment sources, and how to subscribe to *The Finish Line.*

British Flyball Association
Kevin McNicholas
50 Tudor Road, Barnet
Hertfordshire, England
EN5-5NP

Start To Finish Line Seminars
Jacqueline Parkin
6 Monica Road, Site B5
Box 28, RR 3
Elmvale, Ontario
L0L 1P0 Canada

Flyball House League Plans
Marion Brinkman
BRAMPTON OBEDIENCE SCHOOL
9446 McLaughlin Road North, Unit #24
Brampton, Ontario
L6X 4H9 Canada

World Wide Web, the Flyball Home Page
http://www.cs.umn.edu/~ianho
gg/flyball/flyball.html

Internet Flyball List
To register on the Internet flyball list, send e-mail to
    listproc@ces.com
Include the following phrase in your message:
    subscribe flyball (*your name*)
Once registered, messages can be sent to
    flyball@ces.com

Through this list, you can access information on those people currently making and selling flyball equipment.

Internet Flyball Address for the British Flyball Association
kmcn@flyball.org.uk

AMBOR
205 1st Street SW
New Prague, MN 56071 USA
Phone: (613) 758-4598

This is the association for mixed-breed dogs in obedience.

P.A.B.A.
Professional Animal Behavior Associates, Inc.
P.O. Box 25111
London, Ontario
N6C 6A8 Canada
Phone: (519) 685-4756 Fax: (519) 685-6618

Click & Treat Training Seminars
(with Karen Pryor and Gary Wilkes)
44811 SE 166 Street
North Bend, WA 98045 USA
Phone: (206) 888-3737

The Clicker Journal
Corally Burmaster, Editor
20146 Gleedsville Road
Leesburg, VA 22075 USA
Phone: (206) 888-4708

The Clicker List on the Internet
Send e-mail to Click-d@txk9cop
            metronet.com
            Subject: none
            Message: subscribe (*your name*)

RECOMMENDED READING

Karen Pryor on Behaviour: Essays and Research
Karen Pryor. North Bend, WA: Sunshine Books, 1995.

Don't Shoot The Dog
Karen Pryor. New York: Bantam, 1985.

A Behavior Sampler
Gary Wilkes. North Bend, WA: Sunshine Books, 1994.

FLYBALL EQUIPMENT SUPPLIERS IN NORTH AMERICA

Flyball Box & Hurdle Plans
Al Champlain
4204 Goldenrod Lane
Plymouth, MN 55441
Phone: (612) 559-0880
sprigan@ichange.com OR Ian Hogg (i jh@ces.com)

John Grant
2079 Waycross Crescent
Mississauga, Ontario
L5K 1J3 Canada
Phone: (905) 822-6143

K9 Kannon
Skene Design
4843 Jeanne Mance
Montreal, Quebec
H2V-4J6 Canada
Phone: (514) 277-3366

KSE Enterprises
1517 North Wilmot Road, #111
Tucson, AZ 85712
Phone: (800) 226-3983

MAX 200
Dog Obedience Equipment Co.
114 Beach Street, Building 5
Rockaway, NJ 07866
Phone: (800) 446-2920
Phone: (201) 983-0450

FLYBALL EQUIPENT SUPPLIERS IN THE UNITED KINGDOM

Alvah Developments
Phone: +44 (0) 1621 852809

Mr. Owen
Phone: +44 (0) 1869 324511

Andrew or Liz Payne
Phone: +44 (0) 1256 702873

FLYBALL PARAPHANALIA

Drawmea
Jenny W. Kaemmerer
6060 FM 1387
Midlothian, TX 76065
Phone: (212) 723-DOGS
jkaemerer@aol.com

Your Comments are Invited

If you enjoyed reading *Flyball Training . . . Start to Finish* we'd love to hear from you. If you want to comment on any aspect of the book, feel free to do so. Just write to:

Editorial Office
Alpine Publications
225 S. Madison Ave.
Loveland, CO 80537

For a Free Catalog of Alpine Books:

or for information on other Alpine Blue Ribbon titles, please write to our Customer Service Department, P. O. Box 7027, Loveland, Colorado 80537, or call toll free 1-800-777-7257.

Additional Titles of Interest:

201 Ways to Enjoy Your Dog
Ellie Milon
Lists all types of organized activities for dogs, tells you where to get information, how to get involved, and how to condition your dog for competition.

How to Raise a Puppy You Can Live With
Clarice Rutherford and David H. Neil, MRCVS
This book is a "must" for every new puppy owner!
Behavior shaping and socialization for your dog's first year.
Available on video covering two through five months of age.

The Mentally Sound Dog
Gail Clark, Ph.D. and William Boyer, Ph.D.
Canine behavior, training, and development, plus correcting common problems.
Accompanying video series available

Owner's Guide to Better Behavior in Dogs
William Campbell
Learn to understand your dog, communicate in ways he can understand, prevent behavior problems before they start, and much more.

Positively Obedient: Good Manners for the Family Dog
Barbara Handler
Basic training, house training and manners, written by an obedience instructor. Also lots of practical tips on care and responsible ownership.

Practical Scent Dog Training
Lue Button
Training any dog to track for fun, for AKC tracking, or search and rescue.